# Who Are You And What On Earth Are You Doing Here?

bj King

Who Are You And What On Earth Are You Doing Here?
bj King

Copyright © 2025 by bj King

Published by 1st World Publishing
P.O. Box 2211, Fairfield, Iowa 52556
tel: 641-209-5000 • fax: 866-440-5234
web: www.1stworldpublishing.com

First Edition

ISBN Softcover: 978-1-4218-3592-1

LCCN: Library of Congress Cataloging-in-Publication Data

All rights reserved. No part of this book may be reproduced or utilized in any form or by any means, electronic or mechanical, including photocopying or recording, or by any information storage and retrieval system, without permission in writing from the author.

This material has been written and published for educational purposes to enhance one's well-being. In regard to health issues, the information is not intended as a substitute for appropriate care and advice from health professionals, nor does it equate to the assumption of medical or any other form of liability on the part of the publisher or author. The publisher and author shall have neither liability nor responsibility to any person or entity with respect to loss, damages, or injury claimed to be caused directly or indirectly by any information in this book.

I dedicate this book to my dear friends who have supported me during my journey: Judi Rider, Ann Kergan, James Ward, Macy Jozsef, Celia Penman, Marian Sears, Kirk & Marsha Vogel, Marva Wickre, Sandra Simpson, Donald & Lisa Salas, and Therese Scott who have supported me for years.

# PARTNERSHIP AGREEMENT

I, _____(your name)_____, on this date, _____ do enter into an agreement of cooperation with the Holy Mother/Father God of Light.

I agree to recognize The Creator as my Source in all my relationships, both business and personal.

I agree to live from the definition, I AM God expressing itself through the personality of _____(your name)_____, for the benefit of Earth, all life on the Earth and beyond.

I agree to live my life intuitively, asking The Creator at all times, "What is the next single thing for me to do or know to be in a state of Divine Grace?"

I agree to gift a percentage of my monthly income to the physical source who assists me with my personal spiritual growth.

It is my desire to serve the Universe in the following manner:
1.
2.
3.
4.
5.

I choose to be true to myself. I choose perfect health physically, mentally, emotionally and spiritually. I choose freedom. I choose to do God's will for my life.

I choose to serve the Universe with my gifts and talents. In exchange, I accept from the Universe, through the grace of God and to the highest good of all concerned, the fulfillment of my needs and desires.

This contract supersedes all previous agreements I have made with my Higher Self and is duly in force and operating for me now.


Signed:_____ Dated:_____

# WHO ARE YOU AND WHAT ON EARTH ARE YOU DOING HERE?

By bj King

We are here to expand spiritual energy in this dimension.
That is why we have come.
That is our purpose.

We are all here because as souls, we chose to come to Earth. Our hearts beat with the energy of God. We are aspects of God in Human form. In the *Bible* it says we were made in the image and likeness of God, which means we are creators and capable of creating as God does. We were made by God, for God to use and until we understand that, life doesn't make as much sense. God is the Source of our lives. I have found it useful to think of myself in terms of: I AM God, operating through my personality for the benefit of Earth, all species of life on the Earth and beyond. You might desire to write out this affirmation and include your name.

It is not fate, nor chance, nor luck, nor coincidence that we are living at this time. Our births were not mishaps or mistakes or a fluke of nature. Our parents may not have planned us, but God did.

## 1.

# God says there are illegitimate parents, but there are no illegitimate children.

As a teenager, I remember listening to Patty Page's song, "Ke Sera Sera, Whatever Will Be, Will Be," and wondering if that was true. Was my destiny already established and I had no control over my future? I watched stars on TV and movies and read movie magazines and wondered, from the horrors I read about the lives of these people, would fame and success be worth the price of selling one's soul, giving up a normal family life, one's conscience, one's values, and one's dignity? I didn't have successful people around me to emulate or people with whom to discuss these ideas. My examples were from TV and magazines.

In adolescent as I read the *Bible*, Ralph Waldo Emerson and tried to read Shakespeare, I came across sayings that made me wonder even more what was really true: "As one thinketh in his heart, so he is." "Let God transform you into a new person by changing the way you think. Then you will know what God desires you to do." "Great men are those who see that thoughts rule the World." "There is nothing either good or bad except that thinking makes it so." Did it matter what I thought, how I thought?

Later in life, when I actually deliberately pursued reading more philosophers writings and novelists, I came across other quotes that caused me to wonder about success and how it related to one's thinking. Disraeli said, "Life is too short to be little."

Reading Thoreau's "Walden Pond," I came across this which made me really wonder: did it matter not just what I thought, but what I imagined was possible? I read: "I learned that if one advances confidently in the direction of his dreams, and endeavors to live the life he has imagined, he will meet with a success unexpected in common hours. He will pass an invisible boundary; new, universal, and more liberal Laws will begin to establish themselves around and within him; or the Old Laws will be expanded, and interpreted in his favor in a more liberal sense, and he will live with the license of a higher order of beings."

What he describes has actually been my experience as you will witness in my stories. I've learned to live expecting positive exceptions to be made in my favor, and I suggest you also live with this belief. It makes all the difference in our experience.

True success for most of us means personal prosperity: a lovely place to live, vacations, travel, new things, financial serenity and giving help to others. Success means winning the admiration and trust of others. Success means freedom, freedom from worries, fears, frustrations and failure. Success means self-respect, continually finding more real happiness and satisfaction from life, being able to do more for those you desire to help.

Success is determined not so much by the size of one's brain as it is by the size of one's thinking. I've determined by observation that the size of one's bank accounts, how happy a person is, and the size of one's general satisfaction, is dependent on the size of one's thinking. There is magic in thinking big and thinking positively. We are products of the thinking around us, which is why it is important to surround ourselves with positive people, positive thoughts and with very little exposure to media coverage of so-called current events.

Believe you can succeed and you will, cure yourself of making excuses, overcome your fears, think big, dream creatively, realize you are what you think you are, get in the habit of taking action, set goals, write down your desires. Writing down your thoughts and desires is the best way to clarify them. I've included sheets with the word formulas added for you to duplicate and fill out at the end of the book.

To find out why a thing was created, it is best to ask the Creator. As souls, aspects of God, we made a conscious decision to come to Earth to accomplish and to learn certain things. Remembering what that was gives us our purpose. We did not create ourselves, so there is no way we can tell ourselves why we were created or for what purpose. Since it all begins with God, since we were created by God, the place to look for what we agreed to as our purpose for this life is with God. We can communicate with God though our souls in meditation. It is possible to communicate with our souls and with God, directly. This is something I was not taught while I was involved in religion, but something I learned through desire and desperation. Later, it occurred to me that the church hierarchy didn't teach meditation or direct soul communication because it would put them out of business.

## 2.

# Living without a purpose is not as satisfying as living with a purpose.

We can speculate about our purpose but it is only by communicating with God through our souls that we can discover our origin, our identity, our meaning, our true purpose, our significance and our destiny. The larger, cosmic purpose of our lives fits into a much larger plan called "The Divine Plan of God."

We were all born with Freewill as a gift from our Creator, and we put forth a great deal of effort to develop it. From the age of two, when we learn to speak, we respond "no" to most everything we are asked and "mine" to almost everything else, because we believed we were separate and that there is not enough of everything for everyone. We see ourselves as separate from God, The Source, The Creator; and, in our desire for control, we ignore inner guidance. We make hearing inner guidance difficult. For many of us, the idea that "we are one with The Creator" was an idea sparked later in life, if at all. My original belief was that God was outside myself on a throne somewhere judging my actions, and certainly not lovingly supporting me in every decision I made. This belief was offered and erroneously supported by all the organized religions I experienced in my search for truth.

Seldom have we considered any "will" save our own, unless it was our parent's will, or some authority outside ourselves who held physical power over us, such as physical survival or financial serenity. Even though most of us have been exposed to various versions of the Lord's Prayer all our lives, we have either quasi-sincerely or robotically stated "Thy will be done, on Earth as it is in heaven" without really seriously meaning that we were willing to consider any Higher Will than our own.

The question, "What is the purpose of my life?" seldom comes up until our lives are in a heap at our feet. Or:

The World seems to be crashing down around us.

We have managed to engage ourselves in some major health crisis.

We divorce or separate from a spouse or lover.

We experience the death of someone very close to us.

We lose our job.

We lose our home to creditors, to a fire, a flood or it is blown away in a storm.

We experience being burglarized or raped.

Our normal reaction would be, "Why is this happening to me?" But we might also think to ask, "Am I doing the 'right' thing?" Or "What is the purpose of my being here on Earth?"

As long as things are still moving, our boat's not rocking too much and the waves are still manageable, we have a tendency to believe we are in control, and "we" are. One of the aforementioned disasters, however, can bring us to our knees, our bed, our death, or our senses.

My story is not that unusual. I created a lot of drama and self-destruction during my first forty years. I began life in a small West Texas town, married early, did not attend college, found out my first husband was gay, divorced early, remarried, had two wonderful children, fell in love with a priest who was my friend's husband, lost my Mother through a heart attack, divorced again, took the children to live with me and my new love in Oklahoma City, OK. To cope with the drama I had created to this point I had taken four Valium per day for fifteen years. At the time of my Mother's death I began to question, "What am I doing here? Can I live without the drugs?"

When my lover died of a heart attack in my bed on the fourth day of our new life together and the children went back to live with their father in Texas, I began to feel that I wasn't doing something "right", or that I had somehow really made God angry. I was excommunicated from the Episcopal Church by the Bishop of West Texas and the Bishop of Oklahoma because my fiancé was an Episcopal priest and it was the only retaliation the men had to show for their displeasure with my choices. I had angered most of my friends by my choice to go with my heart instead of my logic. I now see that they were mostly angry because they did not have nerve enough to go for what they really desired in life.

I had attended Baptist Sunday school as a child by myself since my family was not religious, switched to Methodism with the first husband

and Episcopalism with the second husband. I was very familiar with God and judgment and not at all familiar with the Universal Laws, God's Love, the Spiritual Hierarchy, the Intergalactic Federation, Meditation or the idea that we are all One and the same energy as God, or the concept that the answers lie within us.

Within my aloneness, where I had no roles to play for anyone (no one's daughter, lover, or wife); I was a mother from a distance, my friends had turned against me and I had no job. I began to think a lot about "Why am I here? How did I get here? What should I do next? Who should I work for? What kind of work should I do? Do I desire to stay on the Earth?" The answer to the last question came back, "Not particularly," which gave me very little enthusiasm for answering the others.

You will note that not once did I ask, "What do I 'desire' to do?" Only the "shoulds" were there. In getting the divorce and moving to live with my new love, I had done what I "desired" and the price and consequences were overwhelming. My family and friends were angry and convinced I had lost my mind. The church officials added their disapproval.

# 3.

# Life is meant to be about letting God use us, not about us using God.

After moving to Oklahoma, my fiancé's death, and the children moving back to Texas, I went back into banking because it was what I knew. I took a bank teller security class while working at Union bank and met the teacher, whose name is David. When David moved to Houston he convinced the people at Oklahoma University, where he had been teaching, to hire me to teach the class in banks all over Oklahoma. The people at OU never asked for my credentials. I took dancing lessons and met another man named David who was an executive at a local Savings and Loan Association; he convinced his superiors to hire me as a bank consultant to create a teller training program for their tellers. It was a time in history when savings and loans were becoming banks.

## 4.

# God does not choose the qualified. God qualifies those who choose to serve.

In August 1982, I finished the bank consulting job with Local Federal. Rather than keep me on as an employee to train their loan tellers to be bankers, as they had promised, I was let go from my job. The same day I was let go from the savings and loan association, I received a call from Peter, a man who periodically came through Oklahoma City on business. He was a very wealthy, older man who lived in California. He had asked me several times to visit him in California and I had always told him I couldn't because I had to work. Well, now I was unemployed and had no excuse. Having been raised to believe men should take care of women, I chose to pursue marriage. I took Peter up on his offer to fly me to California for a ten-day sailing trip on his 35-foot sailboat. He assured me he could sail the boat by himself and that very little would be required of me. Having never been sailing, I imagined lying on the deck reading books while he sailed the boat. I wasn't naive enough to believe there would not be some sex involved, but I was willing. I planned to get Peter to marry me so I would not have to figure out what to do with my life.

I should have been suspicious when the air conditioning in the plane failed on the way to California. It was August. I was wearing a while polyester dress, nylon underwear and nylon stockings. When I arrived in California, I was exhausted and soaking wet from sweat. All I desired was a shower and a nap. Peter seemed excited to see me and our first stop was at a dive shop to get me fitted with a wet suit, because we would be scuba diving off the boat. The wet suit the shop owner offered was still damp from its last user; he offered no talcum powder to make it easier to pull it on. My body was damp and sticky and the suit was damp. I struggled. Cursing under my breath,

"This suit was built for a 14-year-old boy with no ass, unlike me." I waddled out to the show room with the suit hanging down twelve inches in the crotch thinking they could obviously see they needed to get me a larger size. The oriental shop owner made an OK sign with his thumb and forefinger and said, "Perfect." I headed back to the dressing room muttering, "There is no way in hell this is perfect; you must be blind." By the time I got the thing off I was even more exhausted and my arms were aching from the effort.

When we arrived at Peter's townhouse he did not even give me time to take a shower, much less a nap, before he had me across the bed. I stared at the digital clock as he raped me. The man had an erection recovery time of six minutes. I didn't even know this was humanly possible. I wondered if his sexual appetite and endurance were somehow connected to his surviving Auschwitz. When I was finally released to take a shower, I stood in the shower and cried and wondered what I had gotten myself into.

The next morning, before we set sail, Peter took me to The Bodhi Tree, a large bookstore in Los Angeles. He insisted on buying me three books. One on Numerology, one on the *I CHING* and a novel called *A HUNDRED YEARS OF SOLITUDE* by Gabriel Garcia Marquez. His buying me books on subjects I had no desire to pursue made me think him even more strange than I had the night before, but I was determined to see this vacation through to the end and to attempt to get to know him better.

The ten days on the boat were misery. I was seasick. Peter was constantly yelling at me to move, to get out of the way, to hold this or that. When he wasn't yelling at me, he was attacking my body or cooking Hungarian goulash. I knew quickly I had taken myself to hell, but in the middle of the Pacific I saw no way out. On the tenth day I had had enough. I put on the full scuba diving gear, without putting the air apparatus in my mouth, and jumped into the Pacific to kill myself. During the night a huge yacht had anchored next to us. The men on the yacht recognized that the right kind of bubbles weren't coming up where I had entered the water and one jumped in to rescue me. Peter expressed his disappointment in me and we headed back into the harbor.

After unsuccessfully attempting to kill myself, I was ready to give up. The day that I left Texas to move to Oklahoma with Ed, the priest, I went to a Walden's bookstore and bought a book to read aloud to him in the moving van. I did not know the book was metaphysical and I did not even know that word. The name of the book is *ILLUSIONS* by Richard Bach. I read the book to Ed and we both loved it. Years later, the day I returned from California, I noticed it laying on the coffee table with the back cover turned up. I picked it up and read:

*"Here is a test to find whether your mission on Earth is finished: If you're alive it isn't."*

I took the message seriously. I had always been religious, but never really expected God to speak to me personally. I had never totally turned my life over to God because the people I had witnessed in the church who did this went to Africa or somewhere equally foreign to be a missionary and I knew for sure I didn't desire to be a missionary or go to a foreign country. That day I deliberately told God, "I turn my life over to you. If you will just talk to me I will go anywhere, do anything, say anything you want from me."

I expected a big Charlton Heston kind of voice to respond, but nothing happened. No booming voice said, "I hear you" or "go to Africa" or anything else. I decided to go to a book store and look in the Self-Help section to see if anyone had written a book on how to find your life's purpose. As I entered a neighborhood B. Dalton's book store, I walked past the Occult Sciences section. I would have normally avoided anything occult or psychic to the extent that I would have walked around this section of the store because of my inherited and well ingrained beliefs. Psychic and occult practices were religiously taught to be of the devil. This day my depression was so great I forgot my precautions and prejudices and walked right by the Occult Science section. As I passed, a book titled *PSYCHIC ENERGY* by Joseph Weed fell off the shelf onto the floor directly in front of me. Since I was aware that I had in no way jarred or touched the shelf, I was puzzled by the event. I picked up the book and examined the cover. I was not positively impressed by the book. It was a paperback book printed on newsprint paper and the cover was not attractive, printed in red, white and purple and the print was crooked. Everything about the book offended my Librarian sense of beauty and order. I read the back of the book:

### *PSYCHIC ENERGY*

How to Change Desires Into Realities by Joseph Weed

"This is a valuable book, a precious book which you will desire to keep near you and read again and again. It lifts the veil of mystery and superstition that has for too long shrouded the puzzling phenomena so often seen today. In truth, there are no deviations from natural law. Everything that happens, no matter how exotic it may seem, can be explained and understood. Many of these so-called 'wild talents' are described herein and their functions analyzed in simple, non-technical language.

Habitually, we all think in terms of the visible, the material. Yet man is not an animal and he cannot live like one and be happy. On the other hand, neither is he a god so any attempt to deify his higher nature at the expense of his Human heritage is equally doomed to fail. A balance is necessary, and the suggestions given herein will guide you to the attainment of proper harmonium.

In this book you will find information that will surprise and often amaze you. For example..."

I placed the book back on the shelf and proceeded to the Self-Help, Psychology, Religion, and Philosophy sections. I read cover after cover and found nothing that spoke directly to the issue of finding my life purpose. Disappointed and even more depressed, I proceeded to leave the store. As I once again passed the Occult section, I glanced toward the shelf where I had replaced the *PSYCHIC ENERGY* book. To my amazement the book was now lit up. A white glowing light was emanating from and circling the book.

Many thoughts went through my mind. "I am now having a nervous breakdown. I've earned it and this light is proof. Objects don't just fall off shelves and objects don't just light up." Curiosity overcoming logic, I purchased the book and took it home. Still very skeptical, I seated myself on the couch with the book between my hands and said a prayer before I opened it. "If this book is of God I will open it to one page and there will be a message from God." I opened the book in the center and read:

### INSTRUCTIONS FOR INSPIRED WRITING

"If you would like to experiment with inspired writing follow these instructions.
1. "Always take a bath before any inspired writing session. This is not only to cleanse yourself physically of impurities that may be clinging to you but it is also symbolical of a spiritual cleansing which should take place before exposing yourself to any foreign influence.
2. "Sit at a desk or table where you will not be disturbed and compose yourself.
3. "When you are completely relaxed physically, emotionally and clear mentally, take three deep breaths, letting each one out quite slowly.

4. "Then take pen or pencil in your hand, place it on the top line of the blank pad before you.
5. I write "What is the next single thing for me to do or know for me to be in a state of Divine Grace?

"You may get a response the first time but if you don't try again the next day and repeat the preparation here outlined each time. If after a serious attempt, on five different occasions, you get no result, set the idea aside temporarily and try it again in a year when you and conditions about you will have changed.

"When you get a serious response, do not hesitate to ask aloud 'Who is this?' You will, as a rule, get a completely candid answer to this and to any other legitimate question that may occur to you.

# 5.
# Instructions For Inspired Writing From bj

You may want to ask your soul before meditating: What is the next single thing for me to do or know for me to be in a state of Divine Grace?

Deliberately seal this room on the North, South, East and West against any negative influence or entity. I fill this room with the Blue Light of Protection. I deliberately connect and anchor myself through my feet and lowest part of my spine into the Great Central Sun at the core of the Earth. I open my heart in gratitude for my healthy body, mind and memory, Infinite Intelligence, my soul, the Earth, the Sun, the Moon, the Spiritual Hierarchy, the Intergalactic Federation, the Angels, the Elementals of Form, plants, animals, minerals, water, fire and ether.

Send a beam of energy from your heart, through your high heart upward to connect to the Cosmic Christ Consciousness level of your own Oversoul. Deliberately assign this level of your Oversoul to be your Gatekeeper or Receptionist to keep all energies not to your highest good away from contact with you. Intend to communicate with the Spirit World only through your Gatekeeper.

Take a deep breath, roll your eyes upward and hold the breath at the point of the mid-brain activating your pituitary and pineal glands by counting three, three, three and then exhale. Taking another deep breath, eyes rolled upward hold the breath at the mid-brain. Intend to deliberately activate your pituitary and pineal glands by counting two, two, two and then exhale. Taking another deep breath, eyes rolled upward, hold the breath at the mid-brain, to deliberately activate your pituitary and pineal glands by counting one, one, one and then exhale. Count silently, backward from 10 to 1, become more and more relaxed and receptive to receiving information from your soul through telepathy. Do not expect to hear, expect to know what is being transmitted into your right brain through telepathy. Write what you perceive is coming to you from your soul even if it doesn't make sense. Do not censors or need to understand as you write.

Read what you have written when you come out of meditation. Keep what you have written for future reference, it may make more sense later. Thank your soul for this connection and the suggestions of your soul. They are suggestions not orders.

I finished reading the two pages, laid the book aside and made a conscious decision to try this foreign-to-me form of communication since I had asked for direct communication. I took a shower, dressed in a robe, took the phone off the hook, gathered pencil and legal pad, lit a white candle, sat on the couch with my back straight, bare feet on the floor and recited the Lord's Prayer. I began to breathe deeply, becoming aware of my breath as I exhaled slowly.

My conscious mind or, as I later learned, my left brain, my ego, pointed out to me, "This is really dumb. This is the dumbest thing you've ever done. This is not going to work. You should be out looking for a job not sitting here doing such a weird thing. At least put the phone back on the hook so it can ring and on, and on, and on...." I tried to ignore my doubts and continued to breathe deeply. After what seemed like about ten minutes I had another set of words in my mind on the right side of my head separate from the objections and yet still in my own voice:

"Through this pen will come...Through this pen will come... Through this pen will come...Through this pen will come..."

Since I was expecting the writing to be automatic I just kept listening. I'm not a very patient person so after the fourth repetition I asked mentally, "Will come what?"

"The words you need..."

At this reply I began to realize I was to write down what was coming into my head instead of my hand moving automatically, more like taking dictation, inspired but not automatic writing. The words continued:

**September 30, 1982**
**"Through this pen will come the words you need to express the feelings of the World and how you feel about them. I desire for you to now relax, accept, identify and examine your motives for this experiment. This day has been given for your use. It is a free gift. You may, however, be placing a price that I have not required. Try accepting**

my gift without reservation or reluctance. Test this program for thirty days. I will make manifest to you My will for your life and can guarantee you will be amazed at how closely it will parallel your own true desires. Forget all else that troubles you. Choose to accept each new assignment as it appears before you in whatever form it takes, whether a person to be entertained, a task to be accomplished, a chore to be done or a piece of creativity for which you will be given the strength, knowledge, ability and insight to reach a level of awareness you never dreamed imaginable.

"Take this opportunity to reflect...What do you really desire to do? Where do you really desire to be?

"Try this method of putting yourself in contact with the answers to these questions by listening to a pattern of speech coming from your unconscious awareness. If the phone rings, answer with the attitude that you are willing to comfort, be with, or respond to the person on the other end. Create an atmosphere of acceptance for yourself, your faults and your imagined short comings. With my power you have the ability to create, activate and accomplish many marvelous things. I choose you as my instrument of peace to be used by Me in a world that truly needs peace. I will activate in you an energy supply unequaled by any other, my energy, which I give to you this day as a free gift to be accepted or rejected as you choose. I am willing to see you as an equal to me, ready to respond at a moment's notice to the needs of others and, in so doing, be aware that you are not only accomplishing my goals but your own. Now, take your pen and express the feelings I give you in My words and I will reward you with My grace. Try as you will with my love and you will succeed beyond your dreams.

"I have a plan for Our life in you. Give it a chance to materialize and I will reward your efforts by being near you to comfort, guide and direct these efforts in the way for which I have created you to flow.

"This is not a test of endurance, but a test of faith, you cannot fail, you can only stop to begin again. When you feel yourself take control of your life - STOP - examine your results. Do they agree with what you truly desire to do with your life? If not, pause, listen and redirect your thinking to Me and to my words as I give them to you. You are My child and I care what happens to you in this life. I expect you to care what happens, too. This is your life, freely given by Me:

I need your life to accomplish My plan. I am willing to assist in any situation you desire my help. Because you are willing, I can use you for my projection into the World at the Human level. Take My hand as I lead you today and don't fear the outcome; just trust the process that takes us there. We can accomplish things together that cannot be accomplished in any other way.

"Support for your efforts will be made available through an unexpected source and should not be a concern for you at this time.

"Redo your work when you feel you have not pleased yourself, because you are aware of the need for quality in Our approach.

"Accept the things I send as gifts, not questioning why they should be yours. You deserve My love. It is freely given to you as you express it to others. I will create the material needs you have to be fulfilled.

"Right at this moment there is a need that I will make you aware of shortly, to be accomplished as quickly as possible. Now replace the telephone receiver and wait."

Seven pages later I heard no more words and stopped writing to read what had been written.

"My motives?" I felt my only motive was desperation to have answers about my purpose for being.

"**Test this method for thirty days.**" That seemed fair. I apparently could reserve judgment. I had been questioning my sanity, but I knew I would not personally set myself up to do anything for thirty days. This was the only part of the message I knew I didn't make up.

"**I will make manifest to you My will for your life and can guarantee you will be amazed at how closely it will parallel your own desires.**" This line gave me hope that I would not be sent to Africa to be a missionary.

"**Choose to accept each new assignment as it appears before you in whatever form it takes, whether a person to be entertained, a task to be accomplished, a chore to be done or a piece of creativity for which you will be given the strength, knowledge, ability and insight to reach a level of awareness you never dreamed imaginable.**" Somehow, put into those terms, it didn't feel as if I would be asked to do anything weird or anything that I could not do with the help that was seemingly being offered.

I replaced the phone receiver in its cradle and was startled when it rang immediately. The call was from an elderly neighbor who needed a ride to the doctor's office. **"If the phone rings, answer with the attitude that you are willing to comfort, be with or respond to the person on the other end."** I agreed to chauffeur my neighbor to the doctor. As you can imagine, I was in a state of awe and disbelief from my writing experience.

**"What do you really desire to do? Where do you really desire to be?"** This was more difficult for me to define. I had experienced a very limited amount of the World, how could I know what I desired? I wanted to shout again, "If I'd known what I desired I wouldn't be asking you!" More questions didn't seem like a good answer to my original question.

When I returned from my chauffeuring I tried to make a list of what I desired to do:

1. I desire to do something creative. (Thinking but not writing: not count other people's money all day.)

2. I desire to do something that helps people to communicate. (Thinking but not writing: this seemed like the biggest problem in the world to me.)

3. I desire to work at home, in case my children desire to come back to live with me.

4. I desire to do something I can't be fired from. (Termination of employment once in a lifetime is more than enough.)

5. I desire to teach adults.

6. I desire to help people to self-actualize. (I wasn't sure exactly how, but I did know I desired to learn to become all I could be and to do what I had come to Earth to experience and to share that with others. I'd read one book about self-actualization given to me by a chiropractor I had met at a singles meeting it was called *The Magic of Self-Actualization* by Dr. R. C. Schafer. If I'm honest, I was trying to impress God that I knew such a big word.) I remembered the book said: "Every life exists for the purpose of making a meaningful contribution. Without a purpose that is deeply enjoyed, it is not a life, only an existence. To increase pleasure and reduce the time necessary to achieve the goals of our choice is a primary concern for those of us who are non-technical people, who find ourselves in a highly technical society. To meet this end, we frequently spend huge sums on trinkets, gadgets, and a multitude of status symbols only to find that any satisfaction we derive is fleeting. Then somebody suddenly decides that the solution to all ills is to move to a new neighborhood, a new job, a new membership in some organization, or even select a new mate. The result, however, is only old problems in new places. The answer cannot be found in things and places, only in understanding ourselves and Human nature."

I laid the brief list beside my bed and slept soundly for eleven hours.

> *"Nothing in this World is as powerful as an idea whose time has come."*
> — Victor Hugo

The following morning after my shower I repeated the meditation from the day before. The words began almost immediately.

**October 1, 1982**
**"You will now be an artist. Buy a set of watercolors and parchment paper. You will start a greeting card company called bj originals, inc. Use all lower case letters for your name and no periods. Fold the parchment paper in thirds and paint on the front section. In the middle section you will do calligraphy of the messages I will give you. The cards will sell for $2.00."**

I immediately began to argue. "I don't know how to paint. I'm not an artist. I have no education in art. I think you have the wrong person. By creative I meant not boring; I didn't mean I have any talent. I meant I didn't desire to count other people's money all day or work in a factory doing something repetitious. I only know how to do the calligraphy because I took six nights of calligraphy lessons at a Methodist Church before I left Texas. I know even less about creating a business or marketing greeting cards. And I only have $105.00 left in the World." The words continued as if I was not arguing. The message assured me that I could paint, that all I needed to do was to buy watercolors, brushes and a book called *DRAWING ON THE RIGHT SIDE OF THE BRAIN* by by Betty Edwards. I was asked to do the exercises in the book and was told in a meditative state I would be able to allow the painting to happen through me. The next message was not welcomed.

**"Take $100.00 of the $105.00 and open a business account in the name of bj originals, inc. Notify the state that you can no longer accept unemployment compensation for you are now self-employed."**

This advice really made me wonder if this was God. I thought God would be smart enough to know that service charges for a bank account would eat up the money before I had a chance to spend it. I thought I knew more about banking and money than God apparently did.

You can imagine how well I took that suggestion! The advice did not compute to my left brain, my Third dimensional reality. First I explained to the source of the message that it obviously did not understand much about banking and explained that one does not open two checking accounts when one only has such a small amount of money because the bank service charges would eat up what was there. I further explained that I wasn't yet making any money being self-employed. I agreed that when I was making money I would quit accepting the unemployment. Every day for six days the message was identical. I now see that the majority of lessons I have had to learn in this life have been in the area of money and relationships, particularly male/female relationships. Therefore, this has been where my tests of faith or, of necessity, my leaps of faith have been.

I somehow came to the conclusion that I must either quit meditating and listening to the advice or go with the advice. I gave up the unemployment and opened the bank account. I bought the parchment paper, watercolors, calligraphy pens, ink, envelopes, and the book *Drawing on the Right Side of the Brain*. I began to do the exercises in the book and found to my surprise that I was able to sketch and able to do an oriental form of brush work. From the end of the brush would come a flower, with a butterfly suspended over the flower. When you do something you don't know how to do, it is fun to watch yourself do it.

After I followed the suggestions, money began to come. I received a check for $50.00 for my birthday from my father who never before had sent me money or acknowledged my birthday since my Mother's death. I received an insurance refund and then an IRS refund from two years prior. I began to sell the cards to my friends.

**October 2, 1982**
**"Time is of the essence now you have laid the groundwork for what you are to accomplish at this point in your life.**

**"Retreat from all confusion.**

**"Explain your actions to no one.**

**"Walk into the path I have placed before you.**

**"Take time to examine the principles behind the plan you have established. Does it fit your needs?**

**"Reach out to a person whose needs are similar to your own.**

**"Correspond with the party, try to bring peace without allowing your feelings to interfere.**

**"Explain your needs and desires.**

**"Explain what is happening in your life.**

"Talk as freely as possible without emotion.

"Explain where you have been, where you are going and how you intend to get there.

"Retract nothing you have said in the past, for it was all truth as you saw it at that time.

"My purpose will become clearer to you as we progress.

"Do not become afraid.

"I am with you.

"Be at peace.

"Explain nothing to anyone for any other reason than because you desire to. Do not be forced.

"Rescue your feelings when necessary.

"Calm yourself and others.

"Refine your thinking to include concepts that are foreign to you at this time.

"Propose an alternate route for the life you were expecting to happen and feel good when you believe this is My will for us.

"Think about trying a new method of writing that involves putting aside what you have done up to this point and starting over from a totally new perspective. Through this method you can reach the mass of Humanity we desire to touch by your story. Take time now to reread what you have written. Close your mind to confusion. Accept all things as My will. Create a new beginning both for yourself and for the book.

"Treat the material as you would a work of art, trying to experience the time lapse and expressing your emotions to those you encounter as if you were feeling them again. This will be painful, but you are not alone and I care that you are willing to re-experience today all of the feelings of yesterday for the sake of speaking to the mass of Humans who are missing My message and are, therefore, in constant pain.

"Tape your thoughts as you go, attempting to recreate an image of yourself as you were then, explaining in detail what brought you to this point in time.

"Take up your task and prepare to accomplish more than you intended simply because I AM with you this time. You will succeed.

Many of the messages did not make a lot of sense to me at the time they were given; many have later made perfect sense. I had been in the process of writing a book about my life story and my withdrawal from Valium when this message was received. I could never seem to understand where to start the story. At the time the above advice was given, it did not make sense to me; however, seven years later, when I was really emotionally ready to write the book, the directions made a great deal of sense.

**October 3, 1982**
"Think in terms of trying to succeed and you will fail. Think in terms of doing My will and you will succeed.

"Think about today's assignment as closely as possible, be at peace with your surroundings trying to see at all times that effort is not necessary for the result, willingness is necessary. Take time to promote goodwill. Accept the outcome of whatever you are able to achieve with the arrangements that are made for you.

"Trying to adjust your circumstances is futile; adjusting your attitude is preferable. Awareness of circumstances is contradictory to the type of day you would have planned.

"You feel exhausted. You feel less than willing to be available to the people you will meet today, but you are willing spiritually and, therefore, your physical energy will be renewed to maintain the level of awareness we need to accomplish this task.

"Present yourself with the project you have chosen and I will present you with an alternate plan. I do not do this to contradict you or confuse you, but to confirm that you are experiencing an awakening of time to the ...."

At this moment my hand began to move over the page drawing random marks on the page. I allowed the movements, fascinated with the process. Just as suddenly as it had begun the automatic movements stopped and the words resumed.

"This was a demonstration you needed to prove to you that I am using this method of relating to you for a purpose. Think about your needs, account for your actions and accept the possibility that this is altogether acceptable behavior for someone who works to be aware as you are.

At this point I began to believe that I might have become schizophrenic. I wondered if the voice I heard was an alternate personality, an alter ego of me that had split off because of all the traumas and was now leading me down what seemed to me a very unproven path. I asked the source of the writing:"If you really are God and we really are going to do these things together could you give me some kind of concrete sign, like maybe a burning bush to prove to me that I am not crazy?"

The message came:

**"Look for a type of huge triangle atop a configuration of granite. This is where you will begin to experience your walking into another realm of today's time; a time of which you are not now aware. Take time to experience your thought patterns, questioning why you think the things you do at certain times. Things will become clearer as we progress and you have no need to fear the outcome.**

At this time I began to be told to return to my home town and to visit certain individuals whose names I was given. I was told that when I arrived to visit these individuals, I would be given a message for them which I would deliver during the conversation. This assignment was very uncomfortable for me since the names given to me were people who had been close friends before my move from Texas. They were also the very people who had been so angry with me because of my choice to leave my husband and the community. These were very difficult assignments, but I began to trust and much healing was accomplished as a result of my willingness to re-encounter the individuals. The messages were always given to me at the time of the visit and never before.

**October 4, 1982**
**"Observe your thoughts without judgment. Be aware that thoughts are things. Your thoughts become your reality. Everything that exists in your life started as an idea, a thought. All that you have, all that you are, all that surrounds you is a result of your thoughts, ideas, rules, concepts, wishes, desires, fears and beliefs. Your life is also a result of what you have avoided.**

**"You have the ability to change your thoughts and your beliefs and, thereby, change your reality, and thus the reality of the World.**

**"Observe your thoughts, without judgment, and then shift them to thoughts that align with what you desire."**

When I returned from Texas, I received a phone call from David, the man who helped me get the job teaching bank security seminars for the University of Oklahoma. David invited me to join him in Houston for a week while I was unemployed, to rest and decide what I desired to do next. I agreed to go. He sent me a plane ticket. David was now a law enforcement officer and I did not feel comfortable trying to explain to him that I was communicating with God.

The night before I was to fly to Houston, another man, whom I had met at a singles group, called and invited me to join him at a psychic fair on Saturday. I immediately refused, saying I didn't desire to have anything to do with anything psychic, that I thought psychics were little old gray haired ladies who wore shawls and long dangly earrings, burned incense and told people what they desired to hear. He confronted me that I was a bigot and didn't know what I was talking about, that there is a lot more to being psychic than fortune telling and he dared me to go. Being from Texas, I know not taking a dare means I'm chicken. I agreed to meet him at the college where the event was to be held and explained that I needed to take my own car because I would be going to the airport to fly to Houston in the afternoon. I packed and dreaded going to the psychic fair.

The next morning I met Al at Rose State College in Midwest City, OK. He greeted me with a smile and a hug and we went inside the psychic fair by the back door. The first lecture was about Kirlean photography. The presentation was a film, very scientific, very left-brained. I was impressed, but as we walked down the hallway filled with psychic reader booths, the smell of incense filled my senses and I headed for the door and air. Al followed and, as we walked around the quadrangle, I noticed a huge sculpture in the center of the patio. It was my "burning bush". It was a huge bronze triangle suspended by three enormous spires of granite! I almost passed out and wet my pants. I was amazed and then I began to laugh. I had asked for a "concrete" sign. The Source had given me granite. At least this Source has a sense of humor; maybe the "not boring" part of my plan would be more exciting than I had imagined!

In my excitement and amazement I tried to explain to Al what the symbol meant to me. I'm not sure he ever understood exactly what had been happening to me, but at least I knew I was in the right place, doing the right thing and that was a relief, even though I did not fully understand.

We went back inside the auditorium. The first booth I passed was a Silva Mind Control booth where I picked up a brochure. I was handed brochures on Touch for Health and The Course in Miracles. I began to feel overwhelmed with the energy, the confirmation of the configuration and the incense. I excused myself, thanked Al for inviting me and left for the airport.

Arriving a little early for the plane, I went into the airport gift shop to get a gift to mail to my children in Lubbock, Texas. I browsed through the paperback book rack and was intrigued to find a copy of the *Silva Method of Mind Control* by Jose Silva. I purchased the book and boarded the plane feeling excited, but still a little frightened, by what all of these occurrences could mean.

David's greeting was sincere, loving and a blessing. I was bursting to share what was transpiring, but felt our relationship could not withstand the truth of what was happening in my life. Each day while David was at work I read, painted, meditated and wrote. The fourth day of my vacation the message came to return to Oklahoma City immediately to take The Silva Method course. I explained to David that I felt I needed to get on with getting a job, that I was becoming increasingly uncomfortable being unemployed. He understood and although disappointed, consented to take me to the airport.

Returning to Oklahoma City, I called the phone listing for Silva Mind Control. The woman who answered was pleasant enough, but when I asked how soon I could take the course she said, "I'm sorry you will not be able to take it until next month because we are right in the middle of a course. We taught the first half last weekend and will be teaching the next half this weekend."

I was calling on Wednesday so it occurred to me there were two days between then and Saturday so I asked, "Isn't there any way that I could learn what they learned last weekend between now and Saturday and still go into this group?"

She sounded almost offended that I had asked, but replied, "Well, let me think about it and I will call you back shortly."

In approximately 20 minutes the phone rang. I answered and the teacher explained, "When I hung up the phone from speaking to you, I meditated and received the answer that I am to allow you to do as you requested."

I was ecstatic, but concerned as to how I would pay for the course. "Do you accept credit cards," I asked.

"Yes, we do," she replied.

"Where do I need to come to take the course tomorrow?" I asked.

"We will bring the information to you, if that is agreeable to you," she responded.

Surprised, I replied, "Sure! Great! What time should I expect you?"

"Is nine o'clock too early?" she asked.

"No, that will be fine," I answered, gave her directions to my apartment, and replaced the receiver.

For a few moments I sat by the phone in disbelief. Then it dawned on me that the tuition of $395.00 would max out my Visa card. I had been able to function for daily necessities by charging groceries and gas to my Visa card. The fear began to rise again, but I breathed deeply and challenged myself to believe that I would not have made it this far if what was happening was not truth.

When we finally relinquish control and expect the assistance of the Universe, something organic happens. People find themselves assisting us. I re-encountered this instructor seven years later and she commented she had never before or since given a private class. She was still amazed she had made such an exception.

The Silva Method was fascinating to me. I was a ready and willing pupil. I was relieved that the Silva Method of meditation was so similar to what I was already doing except the Silva Method involved counting 3, 3, 3, with the first breath, 2,2,2 with the second breath and 1, 1,1, with the third breath and then sitting quietly and counting backward from 10 to 1. The Silva Method is an experiential method of learning to be either in your right or left brain at will. The method is simple and easy to accomplish. This is a channeled message I received several years later:

**February 2, 1988**
**"Silva Mind Control is currently the most concise and available method to teach individuals to control levels of awareness.**

**"The methods offered in the Silva course are a composite of many modalities and expressions of truth, the truth of inner communication with aspects of self in various levels of one's Oversoul as well as inter-galactic communication. The exercises have been created to hypnotically suggest trust in self-awareness and healing of the body, mind and spirit. The purpose of the repetitive wording of the exercises is to remove blocks in consciousness which have kept the individual in a state of fear and/or doubt about their abilities.**

**"The inner programming which occurs is subjective and causes the consciousness to allow a breakthrough to inner awareness of the power to bi-locate one's energy, to take excursions out of body and into matter, as well as 'mind merging' with others and the Infinite.**

**"The sense of self, which has been developed through the lifetime up to the point of exposure to the method, is expanded to include the Oneness of self with all energy of others as well as Oneness with all life and matter.**

**"This method is highly recommended for breaking the bonds of limited consciousness."**

Once I had completed the course work, I was able to be aware of the inner promptings without having to enter into meditation. I awakened one morning and began painting without getting dressed. The intuition suggested I go to Albertson's, a large drug and grocery store chain in my neighborhood.

I mentally argued, "But it's raining outside, I was there yesterday, I don't have any money to buy anything I need, I'm not dressed, my hair's not done, I haven't showered, I need to paint," I argued. The thought to go to Albertson's continued and would not go away.

Finally, still not understanding, I ran a brush through my hair, threw on my coat over my sweat suit and left without makeup. I'm not the kind of person who goes anywhere without showering, doing my hair and makeup. I drove to the nearest Albertson's store, took a shopping cart and began to push it through the store. I wondered just how weird things were going to get. Could I expect the peas to light up and start talking to me? As I passed the bread rack, a man's voice said, "What are you doing? I haven't seen you in the longest time." Startled by the voice, I turned to see the Rainbow bread man stocking the bread rack and recognized him as having been a customer at the bank where I had worked when I first returned to banking in Oklahoma City.

I was speechless, mentally searching for words to explain to him God had designed a line of greeting cards and I was looking for a place to market them. Instead I simply said "I'm not at the bank anymore."

"I know that," he said. "The question is, what are you doing now?"

"Designing greeting cards," I blurted out.

"Where do you market them?" he asked.

"Well, I don't have a place to market them yet. I'm still trying to find one."

"Why don't you market them here?" he asked, beginning to give me a sales pitch on the number of customers that came into the store daily and the fact that they were open twenty-four hours per day and that they had eight stores in the metroplex area.

"I don't know anything about marketing, I wouldn't know who to talk to; besides, they wouldn't market a handmade product made by one woman in a national chain store like this," I argued for my limitations.

"How do you know if you don't ask them?" he confronted me. "The regional drug manager will be in town tomorrow from Tulsa and he is the person you will need to talk to. Tell me your phone number and I'll make you an appointment to see him. Give me a call in the morning about 9:30 at the North May Avenue store and I can let you know the time of your appointment."

When I started rummaging through my purse for paper, he stopped me by saying, "Just tell it to me, I'll remember." I verbalized the number and walked away in a daze as I thanked him.

I remembered another quote from the book *ILLUSIONS* by Richard Bach: **"Argue for your limitations, and sure enough, they're yours."**

I returned home and painted for the rest of the day with renewed enthusiasm. The next morning I awoke to 10 inches of snow. I called the store Sidney had indicated, contacted someone who relayed that Sidney had not arrived as yet, but they would be glad to take a message.

I waited less than patiently until 11:00 a.m. when the phone rang.

"This is the manager of the North May Avenue Albertson's store you left a number earlier for Sidney Sheldon?"

"Yes, I did."

"Well, he still hasn't shown up, what do you desire me to do with the message?"

Confused, I blurted out, "He was going to get me an appointment with the district drug manager."

"The district manager called and will not be in town this week because of the snow so you won't need to wait around for him." He thanked me for my call and hung up.

I felt really devastated. What had happened? This didn't seem possible after the way the connection had been made the day before. I was furious! I yelled and ranted and raved at God that I did not want to do this. "If the information isn't going to be accurate I don't desire to do this!"

**"Be patient, I'm taking care of it, keep painting."**

"Easy for you to say, you're not down here with all these bills and you don't have to eat, you don't have people wondering if you're crazy because you're not out looking for a job!" I stormed.

**"Be patient, I'm taking care of it, keep painting."**

I didn't find it easy to be creative under such pressure, but I kept painting and waited as patiently as I was able. Ten days later at 10:00 a.m. the phone rang. It was Sidney the bread man; he had remembered my phone number and his promise. "The district manager is in town today, you have an appointment at 1:00 p.m. at the North May Avenue store, good luck."

I dressed as I would for a job interview, created a small wicker rack of sample cards and arrived at the store and the manager's office at 12:55. The district drug manager was a nice man, very businesslike. "Yes, I like these," he said as he read through every card. "We will start them in the store closest to where you live so you can easily monitor them. After we see how they are selling, we will decide whether or not to put them in all the stores in the Oklahoma City area. Take four hundred cards with this purchase order and your rack to the Bethany store. Thanks for coming by and good luck."

I left the store and went immediately to a wholesale greeting card warehouse to check on a rack. The sales clerk showed me a variety of styles that would fit my cards. The least expensive rack was white cardboard so I could paint a logo across the top. The cost was twelve dollars. I bought the rack, took it home, and created a logo. The next morning I took the cards, rack and purchase order to the store. The shipping agent seemed a little surprised to see me standing on the dock, but honored the purchase order by counting the cards and signing the document and handing me a copy. "It will be about six weeks before you can expect to receive a check. Checks are generated from our home office in Salt Lake City. Since you are a new account, that's how long it will take for them to get you on the computers. After that you can expect a two week turn around."

"Six weeks! How could I possibly survive another six weeks?" I thought.

> **"In order to live free and happy, you must sacrifice boredom.**
> *It is not always an easy sacrifice."*
> **—ILLUSIONS Richard Bach**

I began to borrow small amounts of money from my friends to buy parchment paper and envelopes, confident that I would be able to return the money now that I knew how I would be making my living.

I joined a Silva cottage group, a group of Silva graduates who met once a week to meditate together and use the techniques we had learned in the course. The group was very enthusiastic about my cards and the method through which they were created. All six of the members of the group were unemployed and mentally programming to create their perfect job.

One member of the group was a man named Joseph, who had been involved in Silva and metaphysics for fifteen years. I was surprised to see Joseph in the group, remembering meeting him at the Silva area Christmas party six days after my graduation from Silva. I later learned that Spirit's primary reason for returning me from Houston early to take Silva at that particular time was to meet Joseph so we would later be married.

Two weeks into my career of manufacturing and marketing greeting cards, I was pleasantly surprised to receive a call from the district drug manager of Albertson's inviting me to market my cards in all the Albertson's stores in the Oklahoma City metropolitan area.

I was elated until he informed me it would be necessary for me to furnish metal racks, not cardboard ones, inventory the cards and keep the racks full myself.

I agreed hesitantly, wondering to myself how much metal racks would cost and how I would manifest the money.

I hung up the phone and immediately called the wholesale greeting card company to inquire about metal racks with no company name attached.

"What size are your cards, Lady?" asked the dealer.

As I described the dimension of the cards, he began to laugh.

"Are you in luck, I've got a ton of those racks hanging from the ceiling of my warehouse. I ordered them for a guy in 1977 and his company went under before he even picked up the racks, hope you have better luck. Tell you what I'll do, hang on a minute and let me pull the invoice and I'll give them to you for what the price was in 1977." He clicked me on to hold and left me with country and western music blaring in my ear.

While I waited I asked God, "How will I pay for these racks?"

The reply was immediate, **"Write a check, you will have the money before the check gets to the bank."**

I was stunned! I had been teaching bank teller security for two years for the University of Oklahoma, teaching people to recognize people who were passing insufficient or forged checks. I couldn't imagine me writing an insufficient check deliberately. I also knew that if I wrote an insufficient check for more than $700 it was a felony and I could be sent to jail and never be bonded to be a banker again, the only job I knew how to do.

"That will be eight hundred dollars for eight racks. Lady, if you want I can meet you at the warehouse on Sunday afternoon at 1:00 and let you pick them up," the man on the phone broke into my stupor.

"Eight hundred dollars!" I exclaimed.

"That's the best deal you're going to get anywhere, Lady, I can promise you that. What do you say?" he responded.

"OK, fine. I'll meet you at 1: 00 on Sunday, thank you," I answered as I hung up.

Spirit had also suggested that I take another Silva class that same weekend which would cost $285 and it maxed out my Master Card. I did not have any other available monies or credit cards.

I could not imagine that God could create money on Sunday when the banks weren't open and the mail did not run. It didn't leave room for any obvious ways for miracles through computer errors or the mail.

My mind calculated and conjured possibilities and worried how "I" was going to handle my dilemma.

Saturday morning arrived and I attended the first lecture of the Silva Healing course. As I sat listening to the lecture, I felt someone staring at me. I looked across the room and caught the eye of a tall, white-haired, tan skinned gentleman seated across the room. As he smiled at me I felt a sense of recognition although I could not remember where I had met the man before.

At the first break I walked by him and looked more closely and read his name tag. I did not recognize his name. We both smiled.

"I apologize for staring, but I thought I knew you," I said.

"Yes, I know, I've been staring at you all morning," he replied.

Realizing he might think I was trying to pick him up with the oldest line in the World, I blushed and said, "Must have been in another lifetime." I didn't even believe in past lives at this point so I felt even more foolish in making such a statement. I quickly walked away and took my seat across the room.

At the lunch break, I found him standing in front of me. "Can I take you to lunch and let's try to find out where we know each other from," he asked.

As I looked into his smiling brown eyes I realized I did not have enough money left to buy my own lunch, so I agreed.

During lunch we discussed the fact that we were both from the panhandle of Texas, but could not find any obvious places where our paths would have crossed previously.

He explained that he had recently sold his business and retired to pursue his spiritual growth.

"I desire, more than anything, to hear the voice of my Higher Self," he confided.

As a result of his confidence I told him the story of my meditations and showed him the written messages and the greeting card samples. He was fascinated and envious of my obvious clear connection.

At the end of the day's lectures we had dinner, after which I trusted him with my meditation journal to read over night, even though it was the only copy I had.

I slept very restlessly that night, separated from my journal and still unsure how I would pay for the racks I intended to purchase the next day.

"This is fascinating reading," the man said as he returned my journal the next morning.

"Can I take you to lunch again today?" he asked.

"No, I can't,"I replied, "I have to run an errand at the lunch break to pick up the racks for my greeting cards. Thanks anyway."

"When you come back, come and sit with me, I'll save you a seat," he offered.

"Fine, OK, I may be late though," I said.

"I'll see you then," he squeezed my arm as we parted.

I left and met the man with the racks, wrote the check on blind faith. More tense than I ever remember being I returned to the class and took the empty seat which he had saved deliberately for me.

As I took the seat, the man turned to me, grinned and patted my leg under the table, leaving his hand casually on my thigh. Leaning toward me conspiratorially he whispered loudly, "Did you get your racks?"

I was appalled at the volume of his whisper. I suddenly realized due to his hearing aids he did not realize how loudly he was whispering. I felt he had just spoken through a megaphone.

I nodded my head numbly, unable and unwilling to speak.

"How much did they cost?" he whispered even louder.

My body stiffened even more as thoughts of how to get him to hush went through my mind. I was indignant that he would ask such a personal question. I wanted to say, "The price is my business, God's business, not yours. I don't even know you and get your hand off my leg!" I could not speak.

"How much did they cost?" he repeated even more loudly as if I had not heard him; he took my hand under the table, seemingly to further get my attention.

I quickly wrote $800.00 on a scrap of paper and shoved it toward him to try to get him to shut up, to not tell the whole room that I had just written an $800.00 hot check for which I could be prosecuted and sent to prison, never to be bondable again, never to be employable by a bank again.

He looked at the note and seemingly turned his attention back to the speaker. I tried to do the same. Moments later I felt him slip paper into my hand under the table. I took my hand out from under the table to see what his note said. Instead of a note I discovered he had filled my hand with hundred dollar bills.

My body began to shake. Every admonition my mother had ever given me about not taking money from men went through my mind in red neon letters.

"I can't do this," I thought. "I can't go to bed with this man for money. God wouldn't expect me to do that. I really need this money, but I don't want to get it that way! I really need this money."

As the speaker finished, I turned to the man. Speech still almost impossible, I stuttered, "Wh-wh-what is this? Wh-wh-why are you putting this money in my hand. Wh-wh-what do you want?"

"I desire to help you. It seems to me you need it. You need help to do what you're being asked to do," he said.

"Yes, I need the money," I confessed, "but I can't take it from you. I don't know you. I can't borrow it, I have no collateral. I don't know if I would ever be able to give it back, if I will ever make enough to give it back to you."

"Who asked you? I don't want it back. If you send it back to me, karmically, it won't do me any good. When you do get it, sometime in the future, give it to someone who needs it as badly as you do now. Then it will do some good for all of us," he stated. "Before I left Texas for this trip, my guidance asked me to go to my safety deposit box and take out eight one hundred dollar bills and I never carry cash with me when I travel. I never watch TV other than the nightly news, but a week ago I spent four nights sitting in front of the TV watching a mini-series called *The Thornbirds*. I somehow connected to the sorrow of the priest who had fallen in love with one of his parishioners and I cried through the whole movie. My wife was very concerned, because I kept requesting that she leave the room and leave me alone. I think I must have been feeling the feelings of your priest friend and his sadness at having to leave you. I know he desires for me to help you. I realized this morning when I awakened from my dream that Spirit has been showing me an image of you in my dreams for several weeks."

I could not believe my ears. He was actually willing to give me, trust me with the money. My eyes spilled over with tears as he put his arms around me and kissed the top of my head. My body stiffened again with mistrust.

"I've got to go now; it's a long drive back to Texas. Could I have your phone number so we can keep in touch?" I gave it to him and he wished me good luck as he pulled away.

I went out to the lobby and sat down for a few minutes to get my bearings. I recognized one of the seminar participants, an older woman, sitting next to me finishing a cigarette.

"I didn't get to meet you during the weekend. My name is Eva Landrum," the woman said.

I came out of my fog long enough to introduce myself.

"What do you do?" she asked.

"I design and market greeting cards for Albertson's," I said.

"I work at Albertson's," she offered.

"Really, what a surprise," I said.

"What's more surprising is that my daughter designs and manufactures greeting cards also," she added smiling.

"No kidding, where does she live?" I asked.

"She lives in Hurst, Texas, down between Ft. Worth and Dallas," she answered.

"What kind of cards does she make? What do they look like," I inquired.

"Well, they are long and thin, done on parchment paper. The messages for the cards come to her in her meditations," she confided.

By this time in the conversation my curiosity was peaked.

The stranger asked to see my card samples and was amazed herself by the similarities between my cards and her daughter's. The paper and size were identical. Her company was called dr originals, Inc.; mine was called bj originals, Inc., including the similarity of using lower case letters for our names. The messages were almost identically worded, the price was identical.

When we discussed the possibility of my meeting her daughter, she confided that her daughter was facing heart surgery and, therefore, would not be traveling to Oklahoma City anytime soon.

She was very encouraging that she felt her daughter would love to meet with me. We exchanged numbers, with me explaining to her that my car was in no condition to be driven to Texas so I would not be planning to go. We hugged and we parted.

At this point in my metaphysical education I did not know the importance of ending my list of affirmations with the closure: "I accept this or something better through the grace of God and to the highest good of all concerned." Since I did not know this subtlety of manifestation, when I would claim money from the Universe my car was the vehicle used to get me the money from various insurance companies, without my car being repaired.

When I asked for $1,000.00 because my car was in a hail storm, the insurance check was $1,012.00 which I used to survive. When my insurance premium of $286.00 came due, a client accidently backed into the door of my car. Her insurance company paid me $289.00 with which I paid my premium. The engine was by now using almost equal amounts of gas and oil. It would barely make the weekly rounds of the eight stores in the Oklahoma City area.

Quickly, I realized, after acquiring the card market, that God and I had created a monster. No one person was capable of painting, lettering, channeling, inventorying and delivering so many cards. I was working twenty hours per day with almost no sleep.

A week later I was awakened by the phone; it was the man who had given me the money for the racks. "Hello," I mumbled.

"How are you, how's the card business coming along?"

"Not well. They aren't going to pay me for the first cards for six weeks while they get me set up on their computers in Salt Lake City. I'm not getting any sleep, there is no way one person can paint and letter this fast to keep up with racks in eight stores that stay open 24 hours a day."

"Haven't you got your photocopy machine yet?" he asked.

Sleep deprivation caused me to lose my manners completely. I called him everything I could think of in a very loud and rude voice, mentioning that he had obviously never been broke and that I was broke and obviously had not purchased a copy machine which would cost hundreds if not thousands of dollars.

"Calm down, calm down. I'm coming to Oklahoma City tomorrow to see a doctor and I'm to buy you a photocopy machine so you can do the calligraphy of the messages for the cards on white paper and then photocopy them onto the parchment paper and you'll be able to paint twice as many cards."

Once again my thoughts went to what was I going to have to do for him in exchange for this money and help. He wasn't bad looking and had a nice personality. I was exhausted and I really needed the money.

"I'll be arriving in OKC about noon. If you could go out today and pick out the copier that would best serve your needs, when I get there we can have lunch and then go buy it," he explained.

He came to town the next day and he purchased the photocopier machine with more hundred dollar bills. We were standing in front of it after it had been delivered, figuring out how to operate it when he asked, "And how bad is your debt? You said they aren't going to pay you for six weeks and that your credit cards are maxed out?"

"Yes, and my rent and car payment are due and I have no money left with which to buy the paper and envelopes," I admitted.

"Give me your credit cards," he demanded.

I was shocked by his demand, but they were maxed out and I couldn't use them and I figured he was trying to keep me from trying to use them and get myself in more trouble. He took them and left and I thought he went on to see the doctor and back to Texas. I went into meditation to see what the soul desired for me to do next. I was asked to go to Hurst, Texas to do a laying-on-of-hands for the daughter of the woman I had met in the lobby after the Silva healing seminar. I had panicked my way through the seminar, paying little attention to the speaker because of dealing with buying the racks and writing the hot check. I again began to argue for my limitations. "I really don't know how to heal anyone and my car is using as much oil as it is gas. I don't think it is safe to drive it to Hurst, Texas. I'm barely able to make to all of the Albertson's stores."

In about an hour and a half the doorbell rang and my benefactor had returned. He handed me the credit cards and receipts showing he had paid off $4,000 on the credit cards. I began to cry. He also handed me a miniature cassette tape recorder. When I inquired about the recorder he explained that he had been asked by his soul to stop at the Radio Shack to buy it for me and that it was his understanding that I was to write some books and that I would record the information and later type it up or that someone would help me.

I had been asked a few weeks before in the messages to agree to write some books. Again I had argued that I had no idea how to write a book. The message said:

**"Don't worry, Bach will help you."**

The only Bach I knew about was Richard Bach, the author of *ILLUSIONS*, and I couldn't imagine that I would ever meet him. Then, of course, there was Bach the composer and, as far as I knew, he never wrote books and he was dead.

I explained this to the man and he shook his head and said, "I don't know, that is just what I felt I was to do. What are we to do now?"

I quickly questioned the "we" part of what he said, but explained about the possible trip to Hurst, Texas and the condition of my car.

He smiled and said he was on his way to Dallas to visit his cousin who lived there and that he would be glad for me to ride along with him and then he would take me to the woman's house and buy me a one-way ticket and I could fly back the next day. We called Eva and asked her about her daughter and what she thought her daughter would think about my visiting her. She said she had already spoken to her daughter about me and that she was eager to meet me. She called her daughter and called us right back, saying it was acceptable to her daughter for me to come that evening.

The man and I drove to Dallas and had dinner with his cousin. He had mentioned to me that his cousin was a commercial artist and a mediator and that he had at one time been on the national board of directors of the Church of Religious Science, which meant nothing to me at the time. I told him how the messages had started for me. He admitted that he had not been meditating recently, but that after hearing my story he would start again. He mentioned that he had a cousin who lived in California that he thought would enjoy meeting me. I explained the car situation to him and that I was sure I would not be going to California. He said, "Well, just in case I'll give you his name and number."

He wrote down the information and when I read the note I was shocked to see that his cousin's name was Marcus Bach. I asked, "What does your cousin do for a living?"

He responded, "He writes metaphysical books mostly for Unity Church."

"Does he have any connection to Richard Bach who wrote *ILLUSIONS*?" I asked.

"Yes, as a matter of fact, he is Richard's uncle," he offered.

I still had trouble imagining that I would meet either of these men,

When he dropped me off at Diana's house, the man said this would be the last time that we would see or speak with each other; that he knew his personality well enough to know that if he continued seeing me that he would begin to expect sexual favors in exchange for his help. He assured me that his help had been a "God thing" and that he did not want to mess it up.

Diana is the name of the woman who was also making greeting cards. She and I had a great visit. I explained that I didn't capture much of what the speaker was saying at the healing seminar and she assured me she understood that she was responsible for her own healing and that my responsibility was to just bring through the energy. I flew back to Oklahoma City the next day.

I continued to paint and put the cards in the stores. My children came back periodically to live with me. In 1985, my soul asked me to sell the greeting card company. I didn't even have time to run an ad. The afternoon of the request, a woman called and asked if I had ever considered selling the company. She and her partner brought a check for $3,000 that afternoon. It felt a little like selling a child, because I had become so attached to the company.

The soul then asked me to sell everything I owned that wouldn't fit in the car and that I would be asked to travel to various cities and meet specific people whose names would be given to me in meditation. I would be expected to call these people and tell them that I received their name in meditation and ask if I could come by to deliver a message to them from their soul. This is the worst cold call a person can be asked to make. I took my children back to live with their Dad for the summer, sold everything and began to travel. Once the summer was over, the children chose to stay in Texas and I continued to travel as a homeless person for six years.

*"Destiny is the result of two factors, which grow together in the life of a Human being. One streams outward from the inner depths of the soul; the other comes to meet man from the World around him."*
**— Rudolph Steiner**

Give yourself permission to begin to formulate your list, at least mentally, of what you desire to do and realize you may change your mind several times before you are satisfied. I am including the sheets with the formulas that Spirit has given us for manifesting our true heart's desires later in this book.

Some of the questions I suggest for you to ask yourself may seem obvious or absurd. The object is to encourage you to consider all possibilities, not to discount any interest you have, no matter how deeply you may have buried it, or why.

Begin by asking yourself, "Who am I?" Remember, you are not the roles you play for other people - you are much more.

Answer for yourself in this space, Who am I?

Ignorance of our present selves is a primary blockage to an awareness of our purpose, our mission, our destiny. Often it is our past that blocks us physically and psychologically from seeing our purpose. It is helpful to be aware of our past and our inherited belief systems before we proceed to live our destiny.

The first time I ever tried this, I had a page of "I am_____?" I could not for the life of me figure out who I was, if I was no one's daughter, wife, lover, employee, mother, etc. How could I possibly be worthwhile or even "be" without roles? Once I learned that the I AM part of me is God expressing itself through my personality in whatever roles I choose to play with and for other people, it gave me an entirely different perspective. The use of the expression, "I AM," as spoken in English, releases energy from God, our own Individualized Presence, which is our Source.

I remembered from reading the *Bible* that Jesus preceded His important statements with the words, "I AM." "I AM the Light of the World; I AM the Light that Lighteth every man; I AM the resurrection and the life; I AM the Ascension in the Light; I AM that I AM." Also, the Light of the body is the eye (I AM): "If your eye be single your body will be filled with light." I AM is the so-called "lost word." The *Bible* never said that the I AM is our God essence. The words themselves were not lost, but the inner or real meaning, understanding, use and power were lost to the consciousness of Humankind deliberately through the efforts of the church hierarchy.

When you use I (or any form of it as me, my, mine), never use a negative word following it. Our sub-conscious takes us literally.

Enthusiasm means "to be inspired" or "filled with GOD." The word derives from the Greek, "entheos," or "in God." When we are involved in those things for which we have enthusiasm, we can be sure we are involved in part of our life purpose.

Things that excite or enthuse me are...? List as many as you can think of:

1.
2.
3.
4.
5.
6.
7.
8.
9.

Consider what things you've done, or do, which cause you to lose total contact with time passing. This may require you to remember things you fantasized when you were a child, before adults told you what you should believe, want, or do.

Think back to the age of 10-12 years of age. What activities really caught your imagination?

1.

2.

3.

4.

5.

6.

7.

Allow yourself to fantasize without restraint. No one else has to see your lists unless you so choose. Remember to be absolutely honest with yourself. Do not list what someone your age should have or want. Do not list your spouse's desires, society's desires, or what would take care of anyone else. If you have created a standard of living for yourself or your family, do not consider what would maintain this standard of living. If you have minor children, do not consider how you would provide for them. <u>This first list is to be total fantasy, without restraint.</u>

Do not consider your present education, that you are already trained to do one thing, that you have spent years in one field, or that you have no education, that you have no time to take off to become educated, that you have no money to become educated, that you have no desire to sit through a lot of classes.

**God does not choose the qualified. God qualifies those who choose to serve.**

If you want to start your own business, do not consider how you would get out of your current debt or find the funds to create your own business. Use the formula for facing your financial condition offered later in this book.

The details of how these arrangements are possible become the responsibility of the Universe. Your responsibility is to be absolutely honest with yourself about your true desires.

Things I want to be and have never been:

1.

2.

3.

4.

Things I've wanted to do and have never done:
1.
2.
3.
4.
5.

Things I've dreamed about but never thought were possible:
1.
2.
3.
4.
5.
6.
7.
8.

Things I have done in the past that have really motivated me are:
1.
2.
3.
4.
5.

Things I like:
1.
2.
3
4.
5.
6.
7.

Things I'm good at:
1.
2.
3.
4.
5.

What I like to do now:
1.
2.
3.
4.
5.
6.

When I feel really good about myself I'm usually doing:
1.
2.
3.
4.
5.

What needs to be done that I would be excited about doing?
1.
2.
3.

If I could do anything I wanted for one week, what would I do?

What three things do I want people to remember about me?
1.
2.
3.

Finish the sentence: "Happiness is…

What makes you angry?
What do you desire?
A loving relationship?
Being physically attractive?
A satisfying marriage?
Two months' vacation a year?
A chance to be creative?
Making a difference in the World?
Freedom to make your own decisions?
A beautiful home?
Optimal health?
Unlimited travel?
Honesty with friends?
Sensuous sex life?
A large library of personal books?
Peace in the World?
To be treated fairly?
Confidence in yourself?
Influence and power in your community?
High Spiritual experience?
A satisfying religious faith?
Dependable transportation?
Someone who needs you?
Someone to take care of you?
Orderliness in your affairs?
A close-knit family?
Wealth?

What is important to you in your actual work conditions?
To work alone?
Regular hours?
Totally unstructured work day?
Self-employment?
Good supervision?
Having a variety of tasks?
Work in a small organization?
Company benefits, retirement, insurance, paid vacation and sick leave?
Outdoor work?
Opportunity for over-time?

Little responsibility and risks?
Short commute?

What gives you the most satisfaction in your work?
To be excited by what you're doing?
To help others solve problems?
To contribute to society with worthwhile work?
To be recognized as an authority?
To motivate yourself?
To figure things out?
To work within a structured situation?
To think through new solutions?
To have choice of time to work?
To make a lot of money?
To work in a team?
To work out-of-doors?
To be respected for your work?

**Ask yourself: What do I desire to do? Where do I desire to be?**
Ask in your heart over and over and over until you hear yourself beginning to admit what is your true heart's desire. Your heart's desire is also your soul's desire. Do not limit yourself by lack of education or finances…these will come after you have made the conscious decision to admit what you really desire.

Close your eyes and pretend by creating an image of the ideal day for yourself:
Where would you be living?
With whom?
How would you be playing?
Loving?
Being?
Where would you be working? Under what circumstances?

Now open your eyes. How is your ideal different from your reality today?
You may want to keep a journal of your thoughts.
If you find these exercises difficult, you may need to begin by listing dissatisfactions you have in your life; things that you **don't** enjoy, don't desire.

1.
2.
3.
4.
5.

You may need to list what you 'should desire' according to the significant people in your life in order to get clear about your own desires and what has been programmed into you by others:

1.
2.
3.
4.
5.
6.
7.

What would you do if you could do anything you wanted for a year?

Purpose starts with discovering what is needed and desired, then producing it right where you are, in your family, work and community.

For now, my purpose in life is: (Remember, you are allowed to change your mind and your list.)

I think it is important to understand that some of our major purposes are to enjoy life, enjoy Earth, and enjoy being Humans with emotions, feelings, desires and to be creative, to improve where we are. God designed Earth's environment. It is custom-made with exact specifications just so we can live in it. We have a responsibility to care for it. Years ago I read a book called *Bloom Where You Are Planted*. I don't remember who wrote the book, but it was successful enough that it became a slogan on t-shirts and bumper stickers.

This poem by Russell Kelfer sums it up:

You are who you are for a reason.
You're part of an intricate plan.
You're a precious and perfect unique design,
Called God's special woman or man.
You look like you look for a reason.
Our God made no mistake.
He knit you together within the womb,
You're just what He wanted to make.
The parents you had were the ones He chose,
And no matter how you may feel,
They were custom-designed with God's plan in mind
And they bear the Master's seal.
No, that trauma you faced was not easy
And God wept that it hurt you so;
But it was allowed to shape your heart
So that into His likeness you'd grow.
You are who you are for a reason,
You've been formed by the Master's rod.
You are who you are, Beloved,
Because there is a God!

Where we find ourselves is where we begin to question, "What is my purpose?" Not everyone comes with a huge purpose or agenda to be president or to be famous. Most of us came to learn to be more loving, more helpful to others, to be kind, considerate, and attentive to people and nature, to actualize our talents and our minds; to move beyond survivor mode and into living as a creative, successful Human is one of our major purposes. But being successful and fulfilling our life's purpose are not at all the same issue. We could reach all our personal goals and become hugely successful by the World's standards and still miss the purposes for which God created us.

Everyone's life is driven by something. What is driving your life? You may be driven by fear (fear of death, stress, rejection, judgment), problems, pressure, painful memories, unconscious beliefs, guilt, resentment, anger, the need for approval, the desire to be wealthy, be famous, be loved, be successful, materialism (acquiring things or money to feel secure). Self-worth and worth are not the same. God says the most valuable things in life are not things. Possessions only provide temporary happiness.

We are products of our past, but we don't have to be prisoners of our pasts. Resentment always hurts us more than it does the person we resent. Fear creates more and more situations in which we can feel fear. Feel the fear and proceed in spite of the fear.

Without purpose, life is motion without meaning, activity without direction, and events without reason. Without purpose, life can feel trivial, petty and pointless. Knowing our purpose gives meaning to our lives. The greatest tragedy is not death, but to have lived a life without fulfilling our purpose.

Knowing our purpose simplifies our life because it becomes a standard we can use to evaluate which activities are essential and which aren't. It makes making choices easier. It focuses our life, effort and energy into what is important. Always ask the question: Is this mine to do? Is this in alignment with my purpose? This is the only way I have found to have peace of mind. It simplifies my life and removes a great deal of stress. If I live by asking my soul: "What is the next single thing for me to do or know for me to be in a state of Divine Grace?" and follow the guidance or intuition that comes from my soul after the question, I find life flows smoothly with fewer problems, bumps and questions. There is nothing quite as stress-free as a focused life, one lived through purpose. We can be busy without purpose or productivity. It is usually meaningless work, not overwork that exhausts us. Living with purpose causes us to have passion even about small things.

We are not our bodies. We are not our egos. We are Spirits, aspects of much larger Oversouls who have chosen to deliberately come to Earth for this Human experience. We have chosen to come to bring certain vibrations to Earth and Humanity. We have come to experience being encased in the density of physical bodies and then to wake up and remember we are not our bodies. We are spiritual beings choosing to have Human experiences. We are each a spark of God; this individuated spark causes our hearts to beat. Everything and everyone is an aspect of God. We feel fear when we forget this, when we believe we are separate from God. We have come to Earth to allow our Oversouls, larger aspects of God, to work through these bodies for the benefit of Earth, all species of life on the Earth and beyond. These beings, who are not presently in Human bodies, are concerned with what is happening with Earth and Humanity, because everything that happens on the Earth affects everything and everyone in the galaxy, the Universe and beyond, because it is all God. Our mission is to remember and to consciously evolve toward reunification through awareness.

Past generations of souls have come to Earth intending to bring the message that Humanity was destined to progress by sharing and comparing knowledge. Yet, once here, it is easy to forget who we are and the mission. It is easy to succumb to fear, to believe we are the bodies and to forget to use our intuition. It is easy to develop a conscious or unconscious need to conquer, to dominate and to impose our needs and desires upon others and the Earth, because we have forgotten the truth of who we are and why we are here. We develop an addictive identification with our bodies as who we are and listen to our egos rather than our souls. The ego's only job is to keep the body alive so the soul may operate through it. We have given over much more control to the ego than is productive to the accomplishment of the mission.

When we believe it is purposeful enough to just survive and build a better, more secure World for our children and ourselves; we enter the mass consciousness trance, the World of illusion. We expect to be "saved" by government or saved by the return of a Messiah from what we have collectively created through our thoughts of fear and by forgetting who we truly are.

We are not here just to discover a place in the economy, to survive and to find meaning in family and children. We are not here just to live well and to create a more secure World for succeeding generations. We are here to allow our souls to participate through us, to spark remembering our divinity, the divinity of all beings. We are here to promote unification.

There is no one who is unimportant to God. Each of us was created to give expression to the Divinity within us through our personal gifts. There are no unimportant jobs. Sharing our gifts with the World is our purpose, no matter what our job description might be or what our written resume says about us. We are here to minister to Human hearts. If we talk with anyone, see anyone, or even think of anyone, then we have the opportunity to bring more love into the World. We are on Earth to experience love and wonder. Once we understand this, we can understand that if we focus our attention on loving ourselves, loving the Earth and loving all other creatures, we will experience abundant lives. True abundance and peace do not come from focusing on money; they come when we focus on love, peace, wonder and acceptance.

> *"To love what you do and feel that it matters—*
> *how could anything be more fun?"*
> **— Katharine Graham**

We have all had, and may still have; "a job" or we can choose to have "a calling." You can make any job you have your "calling" if you understand your purpose is to be love, be God doing that particular thing through you for the benefit of Earth and all Humanity. Even if we have a job for survival reasons we can make it into a "mission," a "calling", because wherever you are is where your soul has called you to be at this time. The soul has a purpose for wanting your body to be in this place, at this time, with these particular people. If we stay aware and acknowledge the great mystery that is life, we will see that we have been perfectly placed, in exactly the right position...to make all the difference in someone's World.

That doesn't mean you have to stay in a job or relationship you do not enjoy, but it does mean there is a purpose. Be grateful for the job or relationship you have and design the one you prefer. The sooner we identify the purpose and define our heart's desires (write them down on copies of the pages provided later in this book) and choose another future, the sooner the soul will co-create that future with us. When I look at my life today I see it is a fulfilling of the first list I made on the first day I turned my life over to God.

For each of us there is a personal dream waiting to be discovered and fulfilled. We are to dream our dream, invest it with love, creative energy, passion and perseverance. Intuitions, dreams and coincidences are all designed by our souls to keep us on the path to discovering and fulfilling our dream, the dream of the soul. Our job is to pay attention and to follow the clues.

If you could work in any setting, what would it be? What are your ideal working hours? Imagine your ideal workplace surroundings. What do you see? Compare your ideal with what you are experiencing currently. Are there any similarities? What one thing can you change that would make what you are currently doing closer to your ideal? This applies even if you are retired or so wealthy that you do not need to work for money.

We each need to understand our heart's desires so we can live the soul's desires. We cannot make our daily choices in favor of our heart's desire until we identify those desires. Our lives always change in one of three ways: through crisis, chance or choice. The lives we are now living are a result of the previous choices we have made. To have a better life only requires making wiser choices.

**Little choices are important.**
**In fact little ones can often be more life-altering than big ones.**

Make a conscious choice every day to shed the old: old fears, old issues, old guilt, old limiting beliefs, old patterns or habits of eating, drinking or smoking, patterns of responding or not responding, patterns of suppressing anger or resentments or expressing them in inappropriate ways, the old need to compete or resent the success of others.

What are three small choices or changes you could make now, to begin to enhance your life in big ways? Eat less, drink less, smoke less, talk less, listen more, take a daily walk, write a singles ad or reply to one, spend less, read more, write the first draft of a novel or your life story, paint a picture, turn off the television, visit a friend, write a letter, tell someone you love them, smile more, draw the plans for your dream home, begin to trust your instincts, begin to listen to your soul.

We are here to experience joy. If we are not in a state of joy it is because we have unforgiven aspects within our sub-conscious and conscious minds. The path to joy is through forgiveness; first forgiving ourselves and then forgiving all others as if they are ourselves, because in actuality we have called them into our lives to point out some part of ourselves we have not forgiven. Forgive that you have forgotten your divinity. Ask the Holy Spirit to assist you to forgive.

**Ask for the Divine Plan of your life to unfold through joy.**

Being alive as a Human, but not remembering why we are here, can be very depressing and anxiety producing. But once we agree to remember why we agreed to come to Earth at this particular time, there can be a great sense of adventure born within us. Humanity as a whole is evolving toward remembering everything we knew in the afterlife and to make this knowledge conscious on the Earth. If we make that our goal individually - to remember - we become part of the solution, rather than part of the problems happening on Earth.

When we are born into the physical we run into the problem of going unconscious, and through being trained or socialized into the mass conscious reality, we forget where we came from and why we came. We succumb to fear. Then hopefully we awaken one day and question, can this be all there is? Surely there is more to life than this struggle. There are beings from our Oversouls observing us, watching for us to wake up, and waiting for us to ask this question. They are constantly beaming energy into the illusion we have created here on Earth, hoping to wake us up. When a person begins to question, Why am I here? Who am I really? Their intuition will increase due to additional amounts of energy the Oversoul will begin to send into the physical body.

Regardless of the behavior we observe in others, the truth is all Humans are attempting to wake up to the truth of their being, their divinity. The more positive energy we give to them the better the chances are that they will wake up. When we see someone behaving in a controlling, unconscious, vicious or violent manner, sending them the energy of disapproval, judgment and condemnation only adds to their confusion and gives more negative energy to be acted out. When we see someone suffering in this way, be they our boss, spouse, a politician, a child or a terrorist, we have a responsibility to focus on their divinity; not on their action.

I allow Spirit to teach classes through me and often I take dowsing rods and measure the energy of a volunteer person's aura, which will usually be radiating about three to six inches from their body. When I back up and tell them I am going to hold a positive thought about them and once again approach their body, their aura is much larger. I then ask them to hold a negative thought about themselves and I approach their body again and their aura will register almost non-existent. When the whole class focuses positive or negative energy toward the candidate, their aura will expand and contract in relationship to the type of thoughts being projected toward them. If we project negative thoughts toward a politician who is making decisions affecting large portions of Humanity and the World, we are adding to the problem and not creating a positive space around them in which they could wake up and make positive decisions. We can send anyone positive energy by focusing on the spark of light in their heart and expanding it, without agreeing with their philosophy. To anyone we see operating in a challenging way or when we see someone we have a prejudice about, such as obesity, homelessness, tattoos, or other races, we can simply think, "Bless your heart." Then we become a part of the solution.

We have deliberately chosen this physical life experience at this time. Knowing why we have chosen to be here, and what we had planned to accomplish or learn, will enhance our experience of our lives. One of the most deliberate choices we made was to come to Earth to co-create a life of joyful productivity. We came to remember we are not just physical, but are also energetic, magnetic and spiritual. We chose to come to Earth to remember.

**We create our reality by the power of thought,
intention and emotion.**

We can choose to be deliberate co-creators or creators by default. Creation by default happens when we are not clear about our intentions and we let our thoughts run wild without any control or conscious recognition of what we are thinking. The majority of people on the planet today are creating by default. They set forth thoughts that cause creation; they do not understand they have done it, so they blame or credit someone else. If we learn to co-create consciously and deliberately, we can have easy, healthy, joy-filled lives.

Many people have become numb to their life experience because of tuning in to mass consciousness beliefs and what they are exposed to through the news media and television. Exposure to the mass media can cause a person, who is not strong enough to think for themselves, to feel hopeless. Watching the media can cause a Person to begin to shut down their feeling nature in order not to be negatively affected by the violent scenes they witness on the news and in movies. After watching so many buildings and people exploding, a person's perspective of what is real diminishes. Violence begins to be acceptable to the sub-conscious. The feeling nature shuts down. The line between what is real and what is fictitious is blurred. It is important to your spiritual nature and your purpose of coming to Earth not to expose yourself to violence and acts against Humanity. Our feelings connect us to our soul communication. When we numb our feelings by subjecting ourselves to violence, we lessen the possibility of direct soul communication.

Avoiding watching the violence of the newscasts is not sticking our heads in the sand to pretend these things are not happening. It is more difficult to hold a positive thought for and about Humanity if we expose ourselves to the anger and violence displayed as news or entertainment. If an event is yours to know about, your soul will give you an awareness of it.

**Our purpose is to hold the thought of what we desire for ourselves and Humanity.**

When we think of something destructive, we add energy to destruction. When we see something that offends us, like the killing of whales and dolphins or the war on drugs, war on hunger, war on homelessness or drunk drivers, it is not helpful to be "against" anything. We are to never go to war against what we don't desire. Only being in favor of what we do desire will change the outcome. If we think of what we don't desire, because of the Universal Law of Attraction, we give energy to what we do not desire instead of stopping it. Only by being in favor of peace will peace happen. Being "anti-war" does not create peace. Being against World hunger doesn't feed people; only by being in favor of every person on Earth being housed, clothed and fed will it happen. Having a "war on drugs" doesn't stop drug traffic or stop the reason people use drugs; only by being in favor of every person being addiction free and having strong self-esteem will we cause the outcome we desire.

**Focusing our thoughts and emotions on what we don't desire brings more of what we don't desire.**
**This is the Universal Law of Attraction.**

It is easy to get caught up in the conversations of those around us and their emotions. This is particularly true when the people we are with begin to complain about our government or government officials. **We cannot change the behavior of government officials by complaining about their beliefs and actions. We can only change their actions by focusing on what we desire their actions to be, how we desire them to behave.** If we expect them to act in controlling fashions, if we expect them to be dishonest, greedy or self-serving, they will be. Through thoughts and emotions, others can stimulate our thoughts and emotions in directions that are not positive for us. Just as effectively, we can stimulate positive thoughts and emotions in others by focusing our intention and thinking positive thoughts about them. **It is important to hold clear thoughts and emotions relating to what we desire to have as our experience and the experience we desire to see for the World and Humanity.** If we do this, we can hold our beliefs, thoughts and emotions regardless of what is going on around us. But if we accept that what we see or hear is "how it is" and we feel helpless to change it, because of course we are only one person, then the people who appear to be in charge will continue to behave in obscene and self-serving ways. Until we are strong in our desires of how we want to feel and what we want to have as our experience, it is important not to subject ourselves to those who hold and express negative thoughts and emotions. We are too easily caught up in their beliefs of reality.

**Our reality is what we make it through our thoughts, actions and intentions.**

We came to Earth to experience the beauty of Earth and to experience interaction with other Humans, plants and animals in a loving positive manner. We came to make a positive contribution to the expansion of spiritual energy, beauty and love on the planet. We came to remember we are not just physical, but are spiritual beings having a Human experience. We came to remember that we are connected to a soul that is much larger and more powerful than the body we inhabit. What is in the body is not all of who we are. We did not come to just exist or to survive. We came to thrive, to co-create, to self-actualize.

We are here to self-actualize, which means to become all we are capable of becoming. We can accomplish this by connecting deliberately to our souls in order to be reminded by our souls why we came to Earth and what agenda we had before incarnating. Why did we choose these particular parents? So we could learn how we didn't want to be as adults or did we choose people who are stellar examples of parenthood? We chose the race, the parents, and the country for a reason. We wanted to learn. **We are to never stop learning.** We are to always be aware of what we are thinking and why. What we are thinking and feeling are our greatest guides to what we will create. **What we have thought and felt in the past is what has built the life we are currently living.** If we don't like some aspect of the life we are living, we can change the way we think and feel about that aspect by beginning to focus on what would correct this aspect of our lives.

We came to Earth to bring Spirit into matter. Every Human being intended, prior to this physical birth, to be in physical form. We intended to deliberately create by using our conscious thinking minds. We intended to remember we are spiritual beings as well as physical. We came to Earth at this time because, when we were in Spirit, we realized that this time in Earth and Human evolution there would be tremendous energy for co-creation and growth.

The energy that causes our hearts to beat is spiritual energy. The beating of our heart is our connection to our soul. Scientists have been unable to prove the source of this energy. They do know it is electrical, but they also know that it is more than electrical. Physicians can use electric paddles to restart a person's heart that has stopped beating, but it will not work every time. If it is time for that person to transcend the physical, no amount of electrical stimulation will be able to make their heart continue to beat.

We do not learn from words as much as we learn from experience. Words can stimulate thought, which creates action, which creates experience. Until we have experienced a thing we cannot truly "know" it. We send out thoughts. These thoughts create life experiences. Through these life experiences we begin to "know" what we desire and what we do not wish to continue to experience. Even though we have lived before, it is a blessing that we do not remember our previous lives. Not knowing enables us to consciously remain focused on this lifetime and that which we wish to accomplish in this lifetime without distraction.

The soul, the part of us that transcends physical birth and death, does remember all of the lifetimes we have experienced, both physical and in the non-physical. <u>The purpose of each life is growth</u>. The soul realizes that physical life provides great opportunity for soul growth. The soul knows that we are the creators of all that occurs in our life experience. It is time for us to realize this truth and to begin to operate consciously to manifest the experiences we desire, rather than to manifest by default.

# 6.

# Manifestation
# Every Thought Has Creative Power

When we focus on what we don't desire to happen, we give energy to that happening. **When we focus on the lack of something that we desire, we attract more lack, rather than what we desire.** In order to have what we desire, we must focus our thoughts and emotions on that which we desire with intention. Every thought is not equal in its ability to create. The more emotion behind a thought the faster the event will become physical. Therefore, it is important to realize that if we fear or dread something we are calling that event to ourselves. **Repetition of thought, "habitual thought," causes creation even if there is not great emotion behind the thought.** This is why it is important to look at our "habitual" thoughts. What thoughts run through our minds when we are driving, showering, shaving, putting on our makeup? What thoughts do we have when we are not deliberately thinking?

Do we repetitiously think "I want" or "I need?" If so, the sub-conscious mind takes our thoughts literally and believes we want to stay in a state of wanting or needing, since that is what we are asking for. It is important to think literally, since the sub-conscious takes our thoughts literally and works to manifest what we are thinking and imagining. Therefore, it would be more prudent to think "<u>**I desire, intend, deserve and now gratefully accept**</u>," rather than to think need, want or to think about what you lack. We often think we are ready to have something, such as a relationship, when in actuality we have conflicting emotions and thoughts about how having a relationship would change our lives. **Being ready to accept what you ask for is extremely important.** If we ask for something and it appears in our lives, but appears through a source that we don't desire to receive from or through, we can deny the manifestation, believing that God does not know the best way for us to get what we are asking for. This is why it is useful at the bottom of each page of writing out your intentions and desires to place this affirmation:

> **"I now accept this or something better, through the grace of God and to the highest good of all concerned."**

We do not always know what is to our highest good. We don't always think big enough or expansive enough. We don't always understand why a certain person would be sent to help or to serve us. If we use this affirmation, we can trust that the situations we manifest will be "win/win" for all parties concerned.

It is important to have dominant intentions about our lives. If it is our dominant intention to be healthy, wealthy, wise and to have physical, mental and emotional clarity at all times, we are much more likely to have a happy life than if we are filled with doubt, fear, guilt, jealousy, resentment, and greed. **It is also important not to get caught up in trying to figure out the "how" a thing could or will happen.** In doing this, we have a tendency to miss-create. Leave the "how" to God.

# 7.

# Manifesting Relationships

When I first learned about "thoughts are things" and how to manifest what you desire in your life, I began to keep a manifestation journal. This book contains lists of desires I wish to manifest in my life. I had been through three marriages and divorces so I wasn't ready to take on another permanent, live-in, promise to be with you forever relationship. I was homeless at the time and traveling with only the belongings that would fit in my car, but I was lonely. I knew that I was totally committed to do hourly, whatever my spiritual guidance suggested and I knew that a relationship could complicate that commitment. But I also believed that **God is infinitely creative** could come up with a relationship that would work with my current lifestyle.

I wrote out a decree stating that "I now accept a relationship with a male who is not married, who is available, has no ex-wives or children. He is sexual, sensual, romantic and adventurous. He must be healthy and willing to be monogamous for the duration of our relationship. He must be willing to travel to be with me once a month for a four day "honeymoon," wherever God has sent me at that time. He must be willing and able emotionally and financially to fly himself to that location. He will bring champagne, flowers, milk chocolate, massage oil and a willingness to eat at wonderful restaurants. He will make the plane reservations and reservations at beautiful resorts and hotels. He has his own life and does not need me, but desires to love and cherish me and to be loved and appreciated during the time we have together."

At the time I made this list, it was 1986. I stood on top of a picnic table in Rooster Park in the Columbia River Gorge and read the decree aloud to the Universe ending with: "I now accept this or something better, through the grace of God and to the highest good of all concerned."

During these years of traveling I did not stay in daily contact with anyone other than my Higher Self. I did, however, send notes to my children and a few friends to let them know approximately where I would be at any given time. One such friend was David, who I have mentioned before who had moved from Houston to Austin, Texas. I had told him I was on my way to Portland, OR and the number of the family I would be staying with for a few days. I arrived at their home a few hours after making the relationship decree. These people were friends of friends that I had met in Oklahoma City. When I arrived, they mentioned that a man had called and wanted to take me to breakfast the next morning. They gave me his number. I called and discovered that he was the best friend of David. David had called Robert and had asked him to entertain me while I was in Oregon. We went to have breakfast the next morning. He was unmarried (in fact, had never been married), had no children, was more or less married to his job, which caused him to travel continually. He fit all of the criteria I had listed. We spent time together during my time in Oregon and developed a relationship which led to our meeting and spending time together, just as I had imagined, for several years. It worked well for both of us until he was forced to retire from Honda against his desires and he began to drink daily.

In 1990, when I once again had a home base, I rewrote my decree. I made a list of the attributes I desired in a mate. The list contains 85 items. I've been involved in many male/female relationships in my life so I know what works for me and what doesn't. My experience has been that once we make our list, the Universe begins to send "candidates" to see if we will compromise our list.

When I made my list it did not really occur to me, at that time, the real purpose of relationships. On my list I asked to have someone who was financially independent, hoping to attract someone who would take care of me financially so I could do my spiritual work and creative work without having to figure out how to care for myself financially. **I now know that once you make your list it is important to read your list in terms of yourself and to see if you are as developed as what you are seeking in another person.** If you are not, you know where you need to begin to work on yourself. If you are married or in a relationship, **<u>do not show your list to that person</u>**. If it is to the soul's highest good, that person will begin to change to meet the list you have created.

I was living in Albuquerque in 1990, just having ended a nine month relationship in Mt. Shasta, California. Spirit sent me to Oklahoma City for an art show. During that week I met a man who was 82 of the 85 things

I had listed. To a practical person this seems almost too good to be true. Remember, the Universe will send "looks like" candidates to see if we will compromise our lists. In this case I did. I felt the match of 82 out of the 85 things I had listed was as close as I would ever hope to get to my list. Ignoring the fact that he wasn't financially independent and he had no concept of how to manage the small amounts of money he did manifest, I moved to Oklahoma City to be with him. Daily I overlooked the three things he wasn't and enjoyed the 82 things he was. I increased my ability to manifest to include covering his expenses. After three years, I began to resent the fact that he wasn't living up to his potential and that I was working more and more to make up for it. I dissolved our living arrangement.

Later, looking back at the scenario, I realize that I compromised my list because I didn't believe I deserved exactly what I was asking for and I didn't believe a male existed who was everything I had on my list. I also realized that what I did attract spiritually was exactly what I needed in a relationship to cause me to grow in the area of manifestation where I was still weak, which is the true purpose of relationships: to force us to grow.

Since 1993, I have avoided focusing on creating a primary male/female relationship, becoming aware that I do not believe it is possible for me to create something I've never seen. In March of 2005, I once again began to think about the possibilities. I confronted God with my beliefs. "I've never seen a male who is all 85 of the things I've written down. I know I can't manifest something that I don't believe exists. I can't visualize something that I've never seen. If I've never seen an aardvark I can't manifest an aardvark. How can I manifest something I've never seen?"

As so often happens for me, God's answers come through books that light up or fall off the shelves of my library. The next morning after my tirade at God, I noticed a book I haven't opened in many years called *THE PATH OF LEAST RESISTANCE* by Robert Fritz. When I opened the book I opened to a chapter that said: "If you are attempting to manifest something that you do not believe exists – STOP."

"Well, that's not going to get me what I desire," I argued.

The next paragraph stated: "Instead, write an affirmation asking to be healed of your doubt, your fear and your disbelief."

"Duhh, how come I never thought of that?"

The next morning during my meditation and study time, I wrote an affirmation asking to be healed of my doubt that such a male exists, my fear of how having such a relationship would change my life and my disbelief that my having such a relationship is possible. I suddenly remembered how quickly the Universe had previously answered my requests. So instead of asking for a person who fit all 85 of the criteria for the perfect relationship, I asked the Universe to just send an available male, someone to date who would enjoy going out to eat with me, going to the movies and maybe traveling or going to the casino with me. I had witnessed couples together at the casino who seemed to be having a fun time. One of my recent spiritual assignments has been to go to the Indian casinos and to set up a Christ Consciousness vortex in each one that will bless the Indians and the people who come to the casinos.

All day, after writing the affirmation, I felt an impulse to go to a certain casino in the evening. I resisted the message. I only go to the casino with a certain kind of income, never income of the organization or income needed to keep all my financial responsibilities current. In that category of income, I had $12.00. From Oklahoma City one must drive at least an hour round trip to go to a casino. I was not willing to drive that far with only $12.00. Late in the afternoon I was at my bank cashing the $12.00 check. The inner voice prompted again, "Go to Lucky Star Casino." I finally agreed to drive there, much against my better judgment. After the first thirty minutes I was up $200 and feeling better now that I was playing with the "house's" money. I decided to leave my machine to go to the bathroom and to get a drink.

As I approached the entrance to the bathrooms a man came out and literally ran into me. He was an older gentleman and a bit shaky and unstable on his feet. He stepped back but continued to hold onto my shoulders as he looked into my eyes. I recognized him as a man I had dated in 1981, before my spiritual communication started. We were both astonished to be running into each other (literally) after twenty plus years. He was so emotionally moved by the encounter that he had tears in his eyes. He held onto me and whispered questions into my ear. He had developed Parkinson's disease, which caused him to whisper and not to be stable when walking. He asked if I was married or in a relationship and if I was now living in Oklahoma City. He was neither married nor in a current relationship. He was thrilled we had reconnected. I immediately realized how I had compromised my list. He was male, available, would love to go out to eat with me, to the movies, to travel, and we were meeting in a casino. I all but slapped myself for ignoring the Law of Manifestation. I knew better.

When I was 40, someone twelve years older than me did not seem old. At the age of 64, someone 12 years older than me with Parkinson's seemed very old.

One of my other "beliefs," born of experience with men, is that their primary thoughts in relationship to women are sexual. Within the first three minutes of my re-meeting this man, who can barely walk across a room and barely talk, he looked me in the eye and said, "You know I finally got rid of that bed." I could hardly believe it, in his condition it took him less than three minutes to think of me in his bed! I gave him my card and asked him to call me so we could meet in a quieter place to catch up on what had transpired in the past twenty plus years. I knew the meeting had significance and had been arranged by our souls. As soon as I had given him my card and we had parted, I felt as if I energetically had a ball and chain around my ankle. I could feel him thinking about me, wondering when we would get together and what it would be like.

In Oklahoma, we have a free paper called the *GAZETTE*. In this paper, there is a horoscope written by a man in California who is very intellectual, very amusing and very accurate. The week of April first he prints a funny April fool's horoscope for each sign and then under it he writes the real one. The week after this meeting, I read my horoscope. "God noticed you crying in your pillow because he hasn't sent your soul mate. I'm sorry to report God misunderstood and thought you said "cell mate." The real horoscope for that week was, "Write the book you would want to read yourself."

Be careful what you ask for and how you ask. Be sure you are ready. Read your list for your potential partner and see if you are as developed as what you are asking for. The most important thing I've learned in listening and following my soul is to keep my sense of humor. I highly recommend it.

The best affirmation I've ever read for attracting a relationship is from Julia Cameron in her book *HEART STEPS*.

> **"I now accept and draw to me true love...**
> **I draw to myself my right partner,**
> **The soul whose love serves my soul's highest potential,**
> **The soul whom my soul enhances to its highest potential.**
> **I draw this partner to me freely and lovingly.**
> **As I am drawn to this partner**
> **I choose and am chosen out of pure love,**
> **Pure respect and pure liberty.**
> **I attract one who attracts me equally.**
> **I seek and am found.**
> **We are a match made in heaven to better this Earth."**

May you be blessed with relationships that will cause you to grow spiritually through joy, love and adventure.

# 8.

# Manifesting Automobiles

When I left Texas in 1979 to move to Oklahoma City, I had a beautiful yellow, 1977 Buick. I had never had the responsibility of maintaining a car, since my husband owned an automotive garage, so I had no knowledge of how to take care of a car. Within two years the car was using more oil than it was gas and was mortgaged for more than it was worth.

In May of 1985 I was asked one morning in meditation by Spirit to sell the greeting card company that I had been using as my means of income. It sold the same day (the full story was in a previous paragraph). It was suggested that I sell all my belongings except my car, clothes and a few books, because I was going to begin to travel. I was told that each day I would be told where to go and the names of the people I was to find. I couldn't imagine traveling in the car I had. Spirit suggested that I buy a new car. They suggested that it was blue and had five doors and would get 30 miles to a gallon of gas.

When I sold the greeting card company I had used the money to pay off my credit cards. I had no visible means of income. My car was not in good condition and was financed for more than it was worth. The idea of buying a new car seemed preposterous to my logic. I went to a couple of dealers and each time the salesmen were rude and told me I couldn't afford a new car. That week my son broke out in chicken pox. Needless to say, I felt stymied and confused. I yelled at God that if He wanted me to have a new car that He would have to have it delivered to my driveway; I was not going back to any more car lots to be dismissed by any more males. (Tremendous emotion went out with this request.) That day, a letter came in the mail from one of the dealerships I had visited. The dealership had just been purchased by a new owner. The letter was from the new owner who said he had noticed from their records that I had visited his dealership but I had not bought a car and he personally wanted to know why they had not been able to assist me.

I called his personal number and gave him an earful of how rude his salesman had been to me. I explained that after checking the condition of my car and employment that he had dropped me off at the used car lot without even introducing me to a used car salesperson. The owner was extremely apologetic. He asked me what kind of vehicle I was looking to purchase. I gave him the description that Spirit had given me. The part about five doors was still confusing to me. I had never had a car with a hatchback, so had never considered this as a fifth door. He replied that he had that exact car in his show room and he would personally be glad to show it to me. I explained to him that my son had chicken pox and that it would be a few days before I could go out again to look at cars and that I was now considering another brand. He asked me what kind of payment I thought I could manage. Out of my mouth came, "$200." Since I now had no income I thought I was lying. He thanked me and hung up.

Twenty minutes later the original salesperson who had been so rude to me called. He apologized and said, "I don't know what you said to Mr. Smicklas, but he has instructed me to bring the car and the contract to your house as soon as it is convenient for you." He brought the car and contract. I signed it and he took away my damaged car. The contract included the dealership paying off the bank note I had on my old car. I drove this car for three years from one side of the United States to another and back again. When I began to travel, I thought it would be for the three months of the summer and then I would rent another house and the children would come back to live with me. Spirit had another idea. The children chose to stay with their Dad in Texas and Spirit asked me to continue to travel. The truth was, if I was going to continue to travel and live out of my car, I now needed a van, rather than a hatchback.

I wrote out my intention to now accept a blue minivan, with cruise control, cassette player and electric windows, doors and seats. I still had no visible means of income. Shortly after writing my desire and intention, I was traveling through Amarillo, Texas, and stopped to visit with a woman I had previously met there. I did not mention to her my desire to have a van, but while we were visiting she said, "You know, bj, if you are going to continue to travel I think you need to get a minivan." I laughed and told her I agreed with her but that I did not see how, short of a miracle, that it could happen. She pointed out that her father always bought his cars from this one dealer in Pampa, Texas, and she thought if we went to see him, he could help me. Of course she didn't say "father" she said "My Daddy" with a southern drawl. We drove to Pampa and she explained to the dealer that I was a friend of her "Daddy" (who I've never met) and that I needed a minivan. The man did not hesitate; he did not ask about my income, he did not ask how much I owed on the car I was driving. He simply said, "Do you see anything you like?"

I pointed to a blue Ford minivan. He asked if I would like to drive it first. My friend and I drove the car around for a few minutes. All the time we are driving I was in doubt that this could happen, because I had no proof of employment and I was still what is known in the car business as "upside down" in my present car (meaning I still owed more than the car was worth.) When we got back to the lot the owner took us inside to his office. He asked a few questions about where the car I was driving was financed. He filled out the papers himself and made a call to Ford Motor Credit to assure the financing. I signed the papers and drove away in the van. Trading cars, or buying a new vehicle, has always been one of my least favorite things to do. The van I've been driving now has over 100,000 miles on it and it is time to trade up. The car knows this. A friend just backed into the side of it as she was leaving the driveway. I'm expecting another miracle.

One of our main problems as Humans is our logic. Because of mass consciousness belief, our logic will create reasons why miracles can't happen for us. We have a tendency to believe that no matter what we want to do, the money has to come first. We are stuck in thinking in terms of money instead of thinking in terms of energy. We came to Earth to prove direct manifestation, to bring Spirit into matter. When we think of a desire, ordinarily, our left brain will put a price tag on the desire. We are being asked by our souls to begin to think beyond money. We are being asked to go directly to the desire, to think energetically. Raising our own personal vibration and stating our intentions clearly, with a willingness to accept what we desire through whatever means our soul chooses to use to gift us with our desire, is our challenge.

Our first job is to be clear about what we desire and to be clear energetically from doubt, fear and disbelief. Be clear about what is our true heart's desire. Don't ask for what you want or need; ask for your true heart's desire.

# 9.

# Manifesting Employment

The single most important thing about asking for employment is to not see your employment as the source of your supply. Your employment is to be your service to Humanity, the Universe and your soul. For the masses, employment equals income. Truly our employment is to be our means of soul growth. It brings us in contact with the people our soul feels would bring us the most growth. We are to choose something we truly love to do in order that our service is truly inspired. Even if you are retired (Spirit prefers that we think of retirement as a graduation) it is important to have some form of service that we perform.

List what you love to do – not thinking about "how will this make me a living." We are not creative enough to think up a job or service to match all of our talents. We are too stuck in the money aspect of employment. There are so many jobs and opportunities out there that we've never heard of or thought of. God is infinitely creative.

Years ago it was time for my children to go to college and I didn't have the money and their Dad had not created savings for this. I wrote in my manifestation journal, "I now accept being able to offer my children higher education." Within a few days a friend in Arizona called and said he had received in meditation that he was to offer higher education to my children and asked what that involved. My daughter accepted his offer and entered college; my son decided not to go to college. While my daughter was in college she became engaged to be married. Then, suddenly, the groom decided that he would not be good husband material and backed out of the marriage. Shortly, thereafter, my daughter found she was pregnant. She was working as a bartender. The situation seemed overwhelming to both of us. But we sat down and focused on what she really desired. We wrote about her new job with conditions that seemed would be impossible to fulfill even for God.

She needed a new car. We asked that the new job would pay mileage so that she could get a new car. We asked that the job would pay at least $10.00 per hour. Minimum wage at this time was at something just over $5.00. We knew the job would be part time, so that she could continue to go to school, but we also asked for medical benefits for herself and the baby. We asked that she could make her own hours and, if it became necessary, that she could take the baby to work with her. We asked that she could work from home. We asked that she could fulfill this job without having to buy a new wardrobe. Our requests seemed impossible, but we had faith that she was doing what her soul intended and that she and the baby would be taken care of. I agreed to quit traveling for two years to be the baby's nanny.

Within a few short days she received a call from a neighbor of the mother of the baby's father. This person stated that he did not feel that the father was living up to his responsibility and that he wanted to help. He asked her about her intended employment. He knew she had been working as a bartender, because he had hired her to serve as a bartender for some of his backyard parties. He proposed that he would call a company that his company distributed for and ask them to create a position that he felt she would be perfect for. The position would be one of being a liaison between his company and the company they distributed for. He explained that the majority of the work would be for her to drive to each of the fifteen Wal-Mart stores in the Oklahoma City area to only straighten the Edy's ice cream. This job did not involve delivering the ice cream, only in keeping the display straightened twice a week. My daughter is a Virgo; keeping order is one of her most natural skills. He made the call to his connection within the other company and she did not even have to be interviewed. She had the job. They agreed to pay her $10.00 an hour plus mileage. The stores are open 24 hours a day and she could go anytime they were open and, if necessary, take the baby in the grocery cart when she went into each store. They gave her a computer, fax and paid for her cell phone.

We, of course, did not know such a job existed; actually it didn't exist until she described it. The Universe created if for her out of our desires. She did not see the job as the source of her supply, she continued to affirm: God is the Source of my Supply. The medical benefits were provided from other sources and other sources of income came to her. All the needs of the baby were fulfilled. The baby's father is a good father. He has the child every other weekend. When she received her Bachelor's Degree, the company hired her as a full time employee with all benefits.

If we see our employment as the source, God can only send us what will fit through our paycheck. If we see our work as our "service to the Universe" and continue to see God as the Source of our supply, we leave open several billion other directions from which our supply can come.

If we truly understand who we are: "I AM God operating through the personality of _____ (fill in your name) for the benefit of Earth, all species of life on the Earth and beyond," we can begin to think differently. And, <u>as we think, so shall our life become</u>.

## 10.

# Living Our Best Lives

To live our best lives we must first understand ourselves. We can only understand ourselves by listening to what we are thinking. We must understand and admit what we love and what we love to do. If we agree to work at jobs we hate, if we agree to stay in relationships that are not satisfying, if we feel unworthy, we will not be living our best lives. Watching what we are thinking is the beginning of wisdom. To "Know Thyself" is the goal. How can we know ourselves if we are unwilling, or afraid, to listen to ourselves? No one else can tell us what we believe or what we think. Self-knowledge is the key to living our best lives. Our souls love to think big.

Before we can be successful, we must believe we can be. We must believe we deserve success, happiness, prosperity and health. I was only able to do this when I finally found the true definition of myself and learned to believe it. I AM God, operating through the personality of bj King for the benefit of Earth, all life on the Earth and beyond. This is the truth of who I AM. This is also the true definition of you.

The soul created our bodies; they were never ours. Our bodies were created to be instruments through which our soul would have a conveyance - brain, arms, legs, body, to serve the World and Humanity by accomplishing and becoming all a Human being is capable of becoming. Our ego convinced us we are our bodies and that our life belongs to us. The sooner we remember that the body belongs to the soul, and return the control of the body back to the soul, the sooner our lives will be fulfilling. When we remember this fact and begin to listen to our thoughts, the thoughts and beliefs we have inherited from others, the sooner we can come in contact with the truth. I believe having access through intuition, through knowingness, through direct soul contact is imperative to live our best life. Before we seek to know for ourselves and gain this ability, our egos are in control of our thoughts, our actions and our fears.

Soul contact happens through intention. When we begin to remember the idea that the soul created the body for its use and agree to relinquish the ego's agenda in favor of the soul's agenda, the sooner we will find true peace and happiness. Everyone is capable of soul contact. Everyone may experience soul contact differently. The highest level of soul contact is knowingness. To see spiritually is, vibrationally, Third and Fourth dimensional. Spiritual hearing is, vibrationally, Fourth and the lowest part of the Fifth dimension. Most of us came into these incarnations from dimensions higher than the Fourth dimension. Most of us came from the higher Fifth dimension or even higher. Our souls do not want us to vibrationally impede ourselves to spiritual seeing, spiritual hearing; they are waiting for us to ask for knowingness. Your knowingness may be so strong that it registers in every sense of your body and may seem as if you saw, as if you heard, as if you felt with your hands what comes to you in knowingness.

When we begin to listen to ourselves and to sort through our fears and erroneous beliefs, when we agree to turn our will back to the soul, it doesn't mean we forfeit our Freewill. Our Freewill is a gift from God. Our lives were meant to be co-creative lives between the soul and the body. In searching for what it is we truly love, we will also discover what our soul loves. Living our best lives will also be living the life we were created to live. Keep focusing on your heart and asking, "What is my true heart's desire?"

We will find out by listening to our thoughts as to why we may feel undeserving, unworthy, not intelligent enough, not educated enough to be a success in life. Once we check our thinking and our beliefs about ourselves, we can see why we have settled for living little lives. Only you can evaluate your progress. It is important to train yourself to be your own authority, to be self-administered. It is important to observe and to experiment in life. In observing ourselves closely and observing other people, we gain greater understanding of what is true, what is real, what is illusion and what we've been taught that isn't true. Our goal and the goal of our souls is for us to self-actualize, to make the most of ourselves, to become all we are capable of being. We do not serve ourselves or the World by thinking and acting small.

**Knowing how to get information is more important than using the mind as a storage facility for facts.**

Listen to yourself, especially when you make excuses like: why you haven't, why you don't, why you can't, or why you aren't. Many people use their health, their lack of education or intelligence, their lack of luck, fear, they're too old or too young, they use I don't have enough money as an excuse for not living their best life, when in actuality it is usually laziness or erroneous thinking that stops us. Or the fact that we have developed bad attitudes about ourselves and life that stops us. Too many people spend their energy worrying about what might happen, worrying about their health, worrying about money, worrying about what other people think, worrying about what the government's going to do, worrying about their family, worrying about the future to actually be fully present in their own lives.

What really matters is not how much intelligence we have, but how we use what we do have. The thinking that guides our intelligence is more important than how much intelligence we have.

**God does not choose the qualified.
God qualifies those who choose to serve.**

I know this has been true for me. As I've progressed, God has put opportunities in front of me, for me to be a bank consultant, then to learn to paint, learn to start a business, how to operate a non-profit organization, to soul communicate, to do counseling, to write, speak in public and teach.

Choose to become an aware person. Practice staying aware, not only of what you are thinking and feeling, but in observing what is happening all around you. Catch yourself when you get lazy and tune out from what you are thinking, feeling and what is happening around you. Commit to remaining conscious at all times.

Many people are afraid to think big, because they are under the illusion that everything is up to them. They are completely unaware that their soul is there to help them accomplish their goals and desires. When I left banking and began to communicate with my soul I had no idea I could be an artist, a spiritual teacher and counselor. I not only didn't know I could paint; I had even less idea how to market what I created in writing and in painting. As I've progressed, my soul has opened the way to each thing as I would trust and attempt. Much of what has happened is sometimes difficult even for me to believe, because it has been so seemingly miraculous, so synchronistic. But, each time I've followed the soul's suggestions, miraculous connections have happened.

Once, as I was traveling in Colorado, my soul suggested I record some meditations to sell. I had no knowledge of how to record professionally or how to market something like cassette tapes. Someone suggested that I invite a woman who lived in Boulder to lunch, which I did. Over lunch I told her a portion of my story. At the end of lunch she asked me how she might be able to serve me. I had no idea what she did and said I didn't know what she meant. She replied that she owned a recording company and recorded seminars, meditations and music for people and marketed their tapes. I was astounded. She agreed to record the meditations I was being asked by my soul to record and to let me pay her as I sold them. She did not charge me for the recording time in her studio. This kind of thing happens when we listen and become willing to do the thing even if we do not know how to do what is being asked of us.

I had a difficult time in the beginning, because I wanted the soul to be logical and efficient. I wanted the messages to be very specific and I wanted to know more than just the next single thing to do. I wanted to know the future before it happened. The soul was kind enough not to show me the future, knowing it would scare me into stopping. I finally learned that the truth was I only needed to know the next thing, and then the next thing and knowing more than that, I would try to take over and figure out what to do rather than to continue to listen. Each time I would trust and follow the suggestions, even though I couldn't see how it had anything to do with what I considered to be my goals, amazing connections would happen. Well, that's not completely true. Sometimes I would follow and seemingly nothing obvious would happen. At those times Spirit would assure me that the other person didn't follow their intuition to show up. Then, if it was important, the soul would have to rearrange the scheduling so I would connect with that person another way at another time.

I think the most important thing I learned was that the messages were not orders; they were suggestions. Before I turned my life over to God, or the soul, I had fear of what I would be asked to do, of what I would be asked to give up. But, I turned my life over out of desperation and was willing to have God, the soul tell me what to do. So when the messages started coming, I saw them as orders from God and attempted to do everyone without question. I later got so tired and so deeply in debt that I was ready to quit following the messages. That is when the soul explained that the messages were suggestions, not orders; that I had a right to say "no" or to negotiate with the soul by writing out conditions under which I could attempt what was being suggested. I was also given a method of how to get myself out of debt. Within one year, using Spirit's method, I had paid off $26,000 in credit card debt. I didn't believe my soul's method would work, but I filled out the form as the details were given to me. Within a few months someone gave me $1,000 in cash and a woman I had helped previously left me a $25,000 CD in her Will. The formula Spirit gave is on the page entitled Financial Condition toward the end of the book.

Living our best life includes living with financial serenity, not financial security. It is important to realize that there is no such thing as financial security. Money can always be devalued by the government, stolen, mishandled by financial institutions, jobs can be taken away, retirement investments confiscated or devalued. The only security I have found is in learning the Laws of Manifestation: Desire, Intention, Belief, Anticipation and Gratitude. Using the Law of Attraction, I've learned that the higher I can raise my vibration, the faster I can manifest my desires. **Like attracts like.** If my vibration is high, my intention is clear and I show up, miracles happen. Spirit has taught me not to think in terms of how much a thing will cost, not to think in terms of money, but to write down the end result I desire.

In the Fourth dimension, the Law of Manifestation requires that we put our desires in writing in order for there to be a contract between the body and the soul which gives the soul permission to intervene on our behalf. At the top of each page on which you write your desires Spirit suggests we use the following phrase. "I desire, intend, deserve and gratefully accept" followed by a detailed description of the desire. At the bottom of each page it is suggested that we release the request to the soul and the Universe with the following sentence: "I now accept this or something better, through the grace of God and to the highest good of all concerned." The top phrase includes intention, desire, belief, expectation, acceptance in present tense and gratitude, which are all important in manifesting. The bottom phrase gives the soul permission to give us something even better than what we have been able to imagine, since, in my experience, Spirit seems to think we seldom think big enough. I have created blank pages for you to duplicate, with these statements included, toward the end of this book. It is a good idea to make more than one set to share with friends and to use if you expand your desires or change your mind.

In designing our lives on paper, we have a tendency to become clearer about the truth of our heart's desires. I look at them as sending purchase orders into the Universe. When I was designing the location for this retreat center, I had written that the center would have a view of a large body of water. The first property I was shown was across the street from a city water tower. Spirit fortunately has a sense of humor. They were attempting to teach me to be more specific. The actual center has a view of a river.

When we continue to think in terms of how much something would cost, and use that as an excuse not to begin, we are building a fence between us and the manifestation of the desire. Then the soul has to knock down or go around our money fence to bring us to the desire. When we think in terms of the end result instead and leave out the cost, the object, opportunity or condition can appear without money being involved or at the time we will have the funds to accomplish the goal.

# 11.

# Manifesting A Roof

After a couple of years of living in the center, the building needed a new roof. I had no idea how much a roof would cost, which was a good thing, because I wasn't inclined to think about affording it. I just wrote "I now accept having a new roof on the building at no cost to me." I did know that the job would be huge, because there were wood shingles under a composition roof. Both roofs would have to be removed and plywood decking would have to be installed before a new roof could be attached. I kept my focus on the end result. A few days later a young man came to the front door and asked permission to climb onto the roof to see if he could get me a new roof. He and his crew were in town from Dallas, because there had been a recent hail storm. He took pictures of the damage and offered to go to my insurance company to negotiate the new roof. The next day he came back and said the insurance company had agreed to let him put on the new roof at no cost to me.

    My father and my brother are roofing contractors in Lubbock, Texas, and I know what a mess can be made when tearing off and replacing roofs and how unscrupulous some roofers are. This young man's crew came the next day and covered the ground around the house with blue tarps and backed a dump truck into the driveway. They moved every potted plant to the back of the deck and covered the koi pond with a tarp. They accomplished the entire roof in one day, removed the tarps, replaced all the plants exactly where they had been before, ran a magnetic bar over the lawn to pick up any nails and left me with a beautiful new roof at no cost to me. It felt like magic.

# 12.

# Mainfesting Education or Travel

When you wish to travel or to receive further education, it is also important not to think in terms of how much it will cost. It is important to write down where you would like to travel, how you would like to travel (by plane, train or automobile). It is important to accept the degree you wish to accomplish or the subject you wish to master. When my children had reached the age that they qualified to attend college, I did not have the money to send them. I wrote: "I now accept being able to offer my children higher education." Within a week a man in Arizona called me and said, "Spirit is suggesting that I offer to send your children to college, what would that involve?" Even though he was someone I knew, he was not a person I would have thought of asking to do something so huge for me. One of my children chose to go to college. He paid for books and tuition for her to go long enough to receive her Bachelor's Degree.

I've learned that when the soul wishes to have my body travel somewhere, that it is a good idea for me to write down conditions under which I could travel there: A paid plane ticket, someone fun to travel with, perfect ground transportation, sufficient spending money, perfect places to stay, perfect food to eat, perfect clothes to wear, someone who knows the language and customs of the people in the area where I will be traveling. I would suggest the same to you.

Living our best life includes being comfortable, but not so comfortable that we are not willing to change, to risk, to adjust ourselves and our circumstances. Life is about change. The earlier in our lives we get comfortable with the idea and the reality that there will always be changes and learn to change gracefully, the earlier we will feel comfortable in our bodies and in our lives. We can let life happen to us, or we can deliberately participate and co-create our lives with our souls.

I write out my desires in detail in the format Spirit has suggested and I live with only one question:

**What is the next single thing for me to do or know for me to be in a state of Divine Grace?**

When I feel the urge, the intuition to call someone, to go to a certain place, to research a certain subject, to look on my bookshelves for a certain book, to eat at a certain restaurant at a certain time, to go to a different drug or grocery store than the one I usually go to, to write a letter or send a note to a certain person whose name comes to mind, to plan a trip or to take a nap, I make an effort to accomplish what I feel is being suggested. As a result of living this way I have found peace. I can feel I am always at the right place, at the right time, with all I was supposed to take with me. Knowing this and letting go of the fear of rejection, the fear of embarrassment, the doubt that I'm receiving the intuition correctly, the fear I'm not doing something right has brought me proof that my soul and the Universe are on my side. Usually I feel the fear and proceed in spite of the feelings of fear. I do still have difficulty asking other people to help me, but I'm working to overcome this fear. I do realize our bodies respond the same to excitement as they do fear.

We all have talents, gifts to be shared with the World and each other. To be afraid to attempt to use these gifts doesn't serve us and it doesn't serve the World or Humanity. We are required to extend ourselves. Shyness does not serve our souls. Fear does not serve our souls. Self-doubt does not serve us or the soul. Our bodies' response to fear and excitement are the same, so it is often difficult to tell which one we are experiencing. To begin to believe we live in a benevolent Universe is a great big step. When we put out purchase orders, the soul and the Universe begin to respond to our requests. I never cease to be amazed when other people listen to their souls and respond to their soul's request to specifically help me or to support the Namaste Enrichment Center. It is always reassuring to know that other people are listening to their souls and that some of them are brave enough to follow their soul's suggestions. It reassures me that I live in a benevolent Universe filled with Spirits.

# 13.

# Manifesting A Home or Retreat Center

I had desired to have and live in a retreat center for years. I traveled for years as a homeless person going wherever Spirit suggested and was tired of staying with other people and sleeping on other people's couches. Friends gave me a rent free condo in Albuquerque, NM for three months, which was a huge relief. Through the years, different people offered to finance a Center, but they also wanted to tell me how to run it, which was unacceptable to me and to my soul. My friend Judi lived in Denver, CO. She is the secretary of the Namaste organization. One day she woke up and her guidance asked her to refinance her home in Denver and to purchase a place in Oklahoma City for me to use for a home and retreat center. She was brave enough to follow her guidance so we now have a beautiful Center to live in and use for guests. When we make our lists, it is also useful to realize other people are also listening to their guidance and some are willing to follow.

# 14.

# Manifesting Siding

The home for the Center had been repossession by Wells Fargo. They had painted the upper wooden story of the house a terra cotta color that I did not feel matched the brick and every time I drove into the drive I visualized the upper story covered with a light colored vinyl siding. After a few years of living in the Center, the upper story either needed to be covered or repainted. Neither Judi nor I had the money to accomplish this. I wrote out my desire and put a picture of a similar house with the siding beside my phone and energized it every time I answered the phone. At this time in my life, my soul was having me visit many of the Indian casinos in Oklahoma to create positive vortexes to bless the people who go there. Every time I went to one of the casinos, I would see the same man no matter what day or what hour I went. He would always win big so I watched him closely, but never spoke to him.

One day I noticed my siding being put on my next door neighbor's house, which really frustrated me. I asked God, "What part of my address did you not get in my request?"

After a few hours of steaming, I went next door and asked the workers to ask their boss when he came to check on them to come over to my house and give me a bid on what it would cost to have siding put on my house. When their boss showed up at my front door it was the man from the casino. I knew I had the right contractor, but I still didn't know where the money would come from. I followed Maharishi's advice; that the money would come from wherever it is now and kept believing. The man was unwilling to start the job even though I assured him that if he did, the money would come. He said he believed in God and he could tell I did, but he wasn't comfortable expecting God to create money.

A few days later a friend called from Minnesota to say she had been meditating and that there was something going on with me that she was to be a part of. She wanted to know what was going on. I explained about the siding, the man from the casino and the fact that neither Judi nor I had the money. She said she would speak to her husband about loaning us the money. She never called back. A couple of weeks later we were meeting in Sedona, Arizona, for the Namaste gathering, which she and her husband were to attend. When they arrived she was embarrassed that she had not called me back. I assured her I understood that her husband didn't want to loan the money. She said he would have to loan the money to Judi, since she was the owner of the house, even though I would be the one paying it back, and that he didn't know Judi well. I assured her again that I believed the money was on its way. She said, "But he would be willing to buy the house from Judi and arrange the mortgage to pay off the sunroom loan I had and the siding so that I would only be expected to pay the mortgage." They would give me life estate to the property and be one hundred percent responsible for the maintenance, which they did. This is what I mean by "this or something better, through the grace of God and to the highest good of all concerned." They can feel they are doing something to aid me and God and can use the tax deductions. I don't need the tax deductions. Listening to our intuition or for messages from our souls and following those suggestions will cause us to live our best lives.

In our lives we will often find situations where it is difficult to converse with certain people. I've learned from Spirit that a problem can never be solved at the energetic level it was created. When I had trouble with this, my soul gave me a method whereby I would write letters to the Oversoul and Guardian Angel. I've used it successfully several times; once when my grown son came to live with me. He was still drinking beer and smoking pot and his room was a pit. I had recently read a book about Fung Shui, which showed that the room he was in was the direction from which prosperity was to come into my life. I didn't feel comfortable kicking him out. I wrote the letters asking that he would find a place he would rather be. I didn't get past the fourth day of writing when he came home and said, "Mom, I know you may feel like I'm abandoning you, but I have found this place I think I would rather be."

He had met a young man who was moving to China for ten years. The man had just inherited a run down two bedrooms, one bath home from his grandfather and he didn't want to leave it empty. He gave my son a ten year lease, with the proviso that he would fix it up, for $175.00 a month.

In another situation, my next door neighbor died and her grown daughter moved her children and all her grandchildren along with all their dogs into the home. It was a disaster for me. I could no longer be quietly in my front yard or my back yard. I wrote the letters asking her soul to find another place she would rather be. Shortly thereafter, she took the equity out of the house, then let it go into foreclosure, moved to the country and built a metal building for them all to live in. I now have great peaceful, helpful, quiet neighbors living next door.

# 16.

# Letter Writing To The Oversoul And Guardian Angel

You may use this method if you have a situation which needs healing, a condition you cannot solve or a person with whom you have no luck communicating with in the Third dimension. You are allowed to write a letter similar to the one that follows:

To the Oversoul and Guardian Angels of ___(name)_____: I ask for Divine intervention for (my relationship with) (healing for) (the current situation for)_____(name)_____. I ask for healing of body, mind, Spirit and emotion in all dimensions and time frames. Recognizing that I do not fully understand the karmic implications in this situation, I ask the Oversoul and Angels to intervene. I ask for healing from addiction, anger, disease, (etc.). I ask that _____(name)_____ become aware of their true nature, their mission and their Oversoul. It has been promised that if we ask, we shall receive. I recognize that by writing these letters for 14 days, and on the 14th day burning the letters, I am acting in accordance with Spiritual Law. I now release this person and their condition to God for resolution. And so it is.

    This method is the only way for the Oversoul and Guardian Angels to be given a special dispensation to override the person's Freewill for six weeks to positively influence the person's life. You may do this for addicted individuals, but the exorcism would work best for addiction as most addicted people are periodically possessed and not fighting their addiction for only one person.

    This is one of the greatest gifts you can offer another person. You do not have to have their permission to write these letters. You can also write the letters for the Earth or a country, or condition which is present on the Earth.

Write the letters for 14 days. If you miss a day, keep writing until you have 14 letters. When you burn the letters, you release the person to God and ask for the highest good for all concerned. Fire energy assists in transmuting the situation. You may write the letters every 8 weeks, leaving 6 weeks in between to allow the Oversoul to intervene. Many miracles have been reported through the use of this prayer technique. Read your letter and ask yourself if you are doing this out of love for the person or because of your need to control and, if so, redo the wording of the letter and be honest about your motives.

We are now living in the Fourth dimension, which Christians would think of as hell. Earth and Humanity are on our way to the Fifth dimension, which Christians would think of as heaven. The Fourth dimension is filled with all the negative thought forms that Humans have expressed since the late 1930's. When Humans decided to attempt to split the atom, the Spiritual Hierarchy intervened and created an energetic barrier out beyond the Fourth dimension to keep the effects of the chain reaction of splitting an atom from going on out to destroy the Universe. We are living in an embryonic sack of our own ca-ca. The beings that have died in a state of addiction, or with such a low frequency of energy that they could not make it through the barrier into the Fifth dimension are stuck in this dimension with us. This is the reason we see so much addiction. These beings no longer have bodies through which to feed their addictions of drugs, food, sex, power, alcohol, nicotine, etc. The only relief they can get is to attach themselves to the bodies of people who are practicing their drug of choice. Many people are now possessed by these entities. It is very difficult to overcome an addiction when a person is possessed by an entity encouraging them to continue the addiction. Spirit has given the following prayer that we have permission to use to do an exorcism. You do not have to have the person's permission nor do you have to be in their presence in order to perform an exorcism, because possession is against Spiritual Law.

# 17.

# Prayer Of Exorcism

Through the authority vested in me by the Cosmic Christ Consciousness, I deliberately call forth to the energy of the Archangel Michael and the Band of Mercy (*a group of Angels whose job it is to move lost souls out of the astral plane*) to enter the body, home, automobile and place of work of \_\_\_\_(name)\_\_\_ to remove all negative influences and entities. I ask that these energies and entities be taken into the Light for transmutation and that there be no negative side effects (physical, mental or emotional) to _____'s body. I ask that her/his body now be triple sealed (*it is helpful to think of the person in three bubbles of Light – Purple, Pink and White*) against any further invasions of negative forces.

*You may or may not choose to tone the sound OM or AUM at this point to increase the positive energy around you. Amen, Amen, Amen. Thank you, Thank you, Thank you.*

If you fill out these pages your life will improve.

# 18.

# My Financial Condition

To get a clear image of your financial condition, list your current financial indebtedness or responsibilities.

                      Total Balance      Monthly Responsibility

Mortgage or Rent_____
Car Payments_____
Utilities:
Gas _____
Electric_____
Home Phone/Internet
Cable TV_____
Cell Phone _____
Water/ Sewer _____
Subscriptions _____
Bottled Water_____
Equipment Maintenance_____
Bank Loans _____
Credit Cards _____
   Capital One_____
   Chase _____
   CITI_____
   Master Card_____
   VISA_____
   Master Card_____
   American Express_____
   Discover_____
   Department Store_____

Personal Loans_____
Insurance
  Personal_____
  Medical_____
  Life_____
  Auto_____
  Home or renters_____
Taxes
  Home_____
  State_____
  Federal_____
Alimony_____
Child support_____

Other_____

**Totals:**

I now release this indebtedness into the Universe. I now accept its immediate and complete payment through rich avenues of Divine Substance. I now accept being totally debt free through financial abundance. And so it is!

# 19.

# Money, Resources And Income

I desire, intend, deserve and now gratefully accept:

_____
_____
_____
_____
_____
_____
_____
_____
_____
_____
_____
_____
_____
_____
_____
_____
_____
_____
_____
_____
_____

I now accept this or something better into my life, through the grace of God and to the highest good of all concerned. So be it.

# 20.

# Primary Love Relationship, Mate

I desire, intend, deserve and now gratefully accept a life mate with these qualities:

_____
_____
_____
_____
_____
_____
_____
_____
_____
_____
_____
_____
_____
_____
_____
_____
_____
_____
_____
_____
_____
_____
_____

    I now accept this or something better into my life, through the grace of God and to the highest good of all concerned. So be it.

*I now accept and I draw to me true love...
I draw to myself my right partner,
the soul whose love serves my soul's highest potential,
the soul whom my soul enhances
to its highest potential.
I draw this partner to me freely and lovingly
as I am drawn to this partner.
I choose and am chosen out of pure love,
pure respect, and pure liberty.
I attract one who attracts me equally.
I seek and am found.
We are a match made in heaven
To better this Earth.*

Julia Cameron

It is important after you make your list of the attributes you wish to attract in a partner that you read your list in terms of yourself to see if you are equal to and as developed as the person you are describing that you wish to attract. If you are not you know what to work on within yourself in order to attract the person you desire.

## 21.

# Relationships

I desire, intend, deserve and now gratefully accept:

_____
_____
_____
_____
_____
_____
_____
_____
_____
_____
_____
_____
_____
_____
_____
_____
_____
_____
_____
_____
_____
_____

I now accept this or something better into my life, through the grace of God and to the highest good of all concerned. So be it.

## 22.

# Travel or Vacations

I desire, intend, deserve and now gratefully accept:

_____
_____
_____
_____
_____
_____
_____
_____
_____
_____
_____
_____
_____
_____
_____
_____
_____
_____
_____
_____

I now accept this or something better into my life, through the grace of God and to the highest good of all concerned. So be it.

# 23.

# Spiritual Life, Spiritual Gifts

I desire, intend, deserve and now gratefully accept:

_____
_____
_____
_____
_____
_____
_____
_____
_____
_____
_____
_____
_____
_____
_____
_____
_____
_____
_____
_____
_____
_____

I now accept this or something better into my life, through the grace of God and to the highest good of all concerned. So be it.

# 24.

# Communications

I desire, intend, deserve and now gratefully accept:

_____
_____
_____
_____
_____
_____
_____
_____
_____
_____
_____
_____
_____
_____
_____
_____
_____
_____
_____
_____
_____
_____
_____

I now accept this or something better into my life, through the grace of God and to the highest good of all concerned. So be it.

# 25.

# Career – Life Work

I desire, intend, deserve and now gratefully accept a career or life work with these features:

_____
_____
_____
_____
_____
_____
_____
_____
_____
_____
_____
_____
_____
_____
_____
_____
_____
_____
_____
_____
_____

I now accept this or something better into my life, through the grace of God and to the highest good of all concerned. So be it.

# 26.

# My Body – Health – Physical Appearance And Condition

I desire, intend, deserve and now gratefully accept:

_____
_____
_____
_____
_____
_____
_____
_____
_____
_____
_____
_____
_____
_____
_____
_____
_____
_____
_____
_____
_____
_____

I now accept this or something better into my life, through the grace of God and to the highest good of all concerned. So be it.

# 27.

# Education And Knowledge

I desire, intend, deserve and now gratefully accept:

_____
_____
_____
_____
_____
_____
_____
_____
_____
_____
_____
_____
_____
_____
_____
_____
_____
_____
_____
_____

I now accept this or something better into my life, through the grace of God and to the highest good of all concerned. So be it.

## 28.

# Home

I desire, intend, deserve and now gratefully accept a home with these features:

_____
_____
_____
_____
_____
_____
_____
_____
_____
_____
_____
_____
_____
_____
_____
_____
_____
_____
_____
_____
_____
_____

I now accept this or something better into my life, through the grace of God and to the highest good of all concerned. So be it.

# 29.

# Automobile or Transportation

I desire, intend, deserve and now gratefully accept:

_____
_____
_____
_____
_____
_____
_____
_____
_____
_____
_____
_____
_____
_____
_____
_____
_____
_____
_____
_____

I now accept this or something better into my life, through the grace of God and to the highest good of all concerned. So be it.

# 30.

# Children And/Or Family

I desire, intend, deserve and now gratefully accept:

_____
_____
_____
_____
_____
_____
_____
_____
_____
_____
_____
_____
_____
_____
_____
_____
_____
_____
_____
_____
_____
_____
_____
_____

I now accept this or something better into my life, through the grace of God and to the highest good of all concerned. So be it.

# 31.

# Stability

I desire, intend, deserve and now gratefully accept these situations in my life to create a feeling of stability:

_____
_____
_____
_____
_____
_____
_____
_____
_____
_____
_____
_____
_____
_____
_____
_____
_____
_____
_____
_____

I now accept this or something better into my life, through the grace of God and to the highest good of all concerned. So be it.

## 32.

# Creative Abilities – Talents

I desire, intend, deserve and now gratefully accept these talents and abilities:

_____
_____
_____
_____
_____
_____
_____
_____
_____
_____
_____
_____
_____
_____
_____
_____
_____
_____
_____
_____

I now accept this or something better into my life, through the grace of God and to the highest good of all concerned. So be it.

# 33.

# Community – Environment

I desire, intend, deserve and now gratefully accept:

_____
_____
_____
_____
_____
_____
_____
_____
_____
_____
_____
_____
_____
_____
_____
_____
_____
_____
_____
_____
_____
_____
_____
_____

I now accept this or something better into my life, through the grace of God and to the highest good of all concerned. So be it.

# 34.
# Opportunities

I desire, intend, deserve and now gratefully accept:

_____
_____
_____
_____
_____
_____
_____
_____
_____
_____
_____
_____
_____
_____
_____
_____
_____
_____
_____
_____

I now accept this or something better into my life, through the grace of God and to the highest good of all concerned. So be it.

# 35.

# Healing

I desire, intend, deserve and now gratefully accept healing for myself and the Earth:

_____
_____
_____
_____
_____
_____
_____
_____
_____
_____
_____
_____
_____
_____
_____
_____
_____
_____
_____
_____

I now accept this or something better into my life, through the grace of God and to the highest good of all concerned. So be it.

# 36.

# Equipment And Supplies

I desire, intend, deserve and now gratefully accept:

_____
_____
_____
_____
_____
_____
_____
_____
_____
_____
_____
_____
_____
_____
_____
_____
_____
_____
_____
_____
_____
_____

I now accept this or something better into my life, through the grace of God and to the highest good of all concerned. So be it.

# 37.

# Clothing And Jewelry

I desire, intend, deserve and now gratefully accept:

_____
_____
_____
_____
_____
_____
_____
_____
_____
_____
_____
_____
_____
_____
_____
_____
_____
_____
_____
_____

I now accept this or something better into my life, through the grace of God and to the highest good of all concerned. So be it.

# 38.

# Symptons Of Evolution Of The Homo-Sapien Species To Homo-Universalis

Each time Humans have made scientifically unexplainable evolutionary quantum leaps such as from Homo erectus, Cave Man to Cro-Magnon, to Homo sapiens it has been as a result of extraterrestrial assistance. Each time it has been time in the Divine Plan for Humans to evolve, God has sent Emissaries of Light to merge with Humans to cause a hybrid species. Humans are now in such a phase of evolution, evolving from Homo sapiens to Homo universalis. Each time various groups of souls have volunteered to come to Earth to hold larger and larger amounts of the Cosmic Christ Consciousness energies for the collective of Humanity, and to thereby speed up Human evolution, this extraterrestrial inbreeding has caused mutation of the Human DNA.

This evolution requires tremendous changes to our physical, mental, emotional and spiritual bodies. This current process of evolution is greater than any other single jump in evolution previously taken by our species. It is greater than the total of all previous lifetimes on this planet. Our bodies are suffering during this evolution. They will suffer even more drastically if we do not become consciously aware that this evolution is taking place and that we can co-create this evolution consciously. We are designed to be a self-evolving species; we can consciously participate.

When we take a look at history, it does not seem that each generation has seen itself as a continuous part of Human evolution. We talk about the Revolutions, the Ages; Caveman, Cro-Magnon man, the Bronze Age, the Industrial Age, and now the Computer Age or the Information Age, but we do not acknowledge Human's co-creation of these Ages, nor the assistance we have received from the Creators to make these evolutionary jumps. Obviously the ideas for the automobile, the printing press, electric lights, sewing machines, photo copiers, lasers, microwaves, cell phones and computers were gifts to us from higher consciousness to help us deal with the speeding up of the energies of Earth.

In this, the Information Age, we are all being bombarded with more written, electronic and verbalized information than we can cope with, file, assimilate, integrate or disseminate to others. This Age is taking us to a point of mental and emotional chaos. This energetic and informational deluge is actually a gift, because it forces us to focus on our emotions and into confronting that which we have created: chaos – chaos for ourselves and for the Earth. Scientists are now looking to find order even in the chaos.

For eons, Earth's systems have been condensing into matter. We have now turned a corner cosmically into our systems moving back toward Source, Spirit and non-physicality. A massive planetary shift is taking place. All of Earth's systems and occupants are becoming less physically dense. Our systems do not understand this change either physically, psychologically, mentally or emotionally. The Spiritual Hierarchy has begun removing the veils, which made it possible for us to believe in our separation from Spirit and from God. More Light is being intentionally beamed at Earth and as those veils are lifted, more light reaches the Earth. As these veils are lifted, we experience more knowingness, more love, and we suspect, more graphically, that we are part of Oneness, that all life is symbiotic.

We are receiving much help from our brothers and sisters in other dimensions and from other systems, as well as from the Spiritual Hierarchy and the Angelic Kingdom. In order to more personally understand our own evolution we must, however, ask our souls for insights and personal direction, personal meaning. This evolution is not happening against our Freewill. We agreed to this process before entering the Earth plane. We agreed to come into a system, which allows fear, pain, suffering, denial, separation, abandonment, death and destruction. At the core of ourselves we feel abandoned. The only way to overcome this abandonment feeling is to reconnect, consciously, to our souls, to actually experience the help that is available to us.

We agreed to come into the system and to forget who we truly are, in order to fully experience the system and what it is to be fully Human. Then we agreed to begin to remember who we truly are and to bring the "system" – to evolve the system – into a new form. We agreed to "be" the evolution, which transmutes the patterns of distortion, fear and greed. This transmutation is taking place in every cell of our bodies. The information was encoded into our DNA prior to our embodiment. The energies, which are now coming onto the Earth, are activating these encoded memories. Others who have come onto the planet more recently have brought with them keys and DNA codes, which help to unlock our own. When we encounter them, we know something has happened to us. We may or may not recognize this as a DNA change. We are each changing at different rates. We each have different functions and designs. It is inappropriate for us to compare ourselves with others. It is totally appropriate for us to communicate with our souls to learn what we, personally, are supposed to be doing to evolve the planet and ourselves.

There is a "quickening" taking place. These changes directly affect all our bodies. Our physical body is a direct outward manifestation of our ether or our energy bodies. Our ether bodies are vibrating at a faster rate. Our physical bodies are trying to catch up and seemingly failing miserably. Our bodies, our blood, our glandular systems, our nervous systems, our skin, our muscles and all our organs are trying to maintain stable conditions with this tremendous influx of energy. They are in a state of overload and confusion.

The infusions of energy are requiring that our souls completely rewire our bodies and nervous systems. Our endocrine systems and organs are, of necessity, being totally reconstructed. These changes are causing many physical, emotional and psychological symptoms. Due to these changes, the bodies are in a constant state of "fight or flight," total adrenalin overload. Our bodies require totally different diets, vitamin supplements and, in many cases, hormonal and thyroid supplements.

The only way to know what we need nutritionally is to tune in to our bodies, our souls and ask for guidance. Each person's needs will be different; however, it is a fact that the energies, which are now pouring through our bodies are burning up the calcium, potassium, magnesium, zinc and iron.

Spirit has indicated that the ingestion of the grain Quinoa will do much to make it possible for our cells to hold more Light. This grain is grown in the highest elevations of the Andes and is available in health food stores. It has very little taste, but can be mixed with other foods. I cook it with stir-fried onions, carrots, garlic and celery with a little cumin added, which gives it a wonderful flavor. The enzymatic reaction of grated carrots, mixed with pineapple and raisins is beneficial to strengthen our cell walls to hold more Light. Drinking coconut juice and eating mangos is also recommended for the same purpose.

Our way of coping with so much energy and tremendous volumes of information, knowledge and sound bombardment has been to turn to specialization. Yet specialization causes separation. We separate ourselves from others to lessen the inflow of information and stimulus. Most people do not know why they are feeling fear or are running away from relationships. Avoidance is our only known way of coping. We and the Earth are floating in a vat filled with the energies of negative thoughts and emotions. We are in the midst of the Fourth dimension. The Fourth dimension is filled with all the negative thought forms ever projected by Humanity. This is why many are feeling free-floating anxiety and non-specific fear. We are used to being able to fall back on our knowledge of Universal Law as it affects the Third dimension. We still believe if we work longer and faster we will be able to keep up with our lives. We do not, as yet, understand how Universal Law affects the Fourth and Fifth dimensional frequencies with which we are now subjected. Those who have been operating empathically are the most negatively affected by these changes. Those of us, who are open and have developed our sensitivity, if we are still operating empathically, are feeling the most pain and effects from this collective negative bombardment. This is driving many sensitive people to commit suicide, live on drugs, alcohol and other addictive substances. Unless we understand these energy dynamics, we will have a tendency to over-indulge in smoking, food and sex to try to ground ourselves and feel in our bodies.

We are feeling chaos and ungroundedness because the vibrations of Earth and Humanity are being continually speeded up. These energies are being deliberately sent to Earth by the Source through the Rays and the Spiritual Hierarchy in order to speed up the evolution of Earth and of Humanity. Earth is moving into the Fifth dimension. Humans may go with Her by raising their vibrations or they may leave the planet. That is the choice we are given. The Earth will evolve with or without us. This is the first time in Earth's history that this type of vibrational change has been accomplished while the planet has been inhabited. This experiment has attracted the attention of 47 different civilizations beyond Earth and these civilizations, who are members of the Intergalactic Federation, are moving close to Earth to assist Earth and Humanity in this evolutionary jump. They are not visible to us because they operate in a higher dimension; only occasionally do they allow their ships to be seen by Humans.

It is time for us to realize that we can actively assist in the evolution, because we ARE the evolution of Humanity. Very few individuals understand this and are consciously participating in this evolution. It is time for us to become conscious that we are co-creators of our species. It is time for us to consciously participate, and to work in concert with the Creators of our planet and our species to bring us and the Earth into alignment with the Divine Plan.

The problems we have created on the planet can become a gift, not just a challenge, if we change our attitudes and our focus. If we turn our focus within ourselves to our "heart knowing," this chaos can be our greatest gift, if it can successfully force us to seek communication with the Creator, learn "The Plan" and take advice from our souls to heal both ourselves and the Earth. We can learn to consciously evolve the Earth, the Human species and ourselves as we were designed to do.

Many of us are experiencing the physical symptoms of intense cravings for certain food, many of which we may not normally eat, unexplained weight gain or loss, sluggishness, altered sleep patterns, having huge appetites one day and none the next, sleeping more hours than usual, having to take naps, or feeling we need almost no sleep at all. Many of us are periodically feeling more tired and fatigued than usual without having exerted physical effort. The exhaustion comes on for no apparent reason. Exhaustion is explainable if we recognize that every cell of our bodies is changing. We are remodeling and rebuilding our entire design. When the exhaustion hits, it is important to acknowledge what is happening – to rest, read, watch calming movies, spend as much time as possible in or near water and nature, garden and communicate with the Devic Kingdom; Devas are Angels who are responsible for all animal, plant and mineral life on Earth. It is recommended that we drink huge quantities of water. Seek the help of body workers, massage, neuromuscular therapy, connective tissue work, chiropractic adjustments, osteopathic assistance, flower and gem essence therapy, homeopathic, naturopathic and acupuncture – all can be helpful. To live comfortably during this time we must honor what is taking place in our bodies and with the species and live in alignment with the evolution.

Psychologically, we are more apt to feel tense, irritable, angry and out of sync, disjointed from what is going on around us or from the demands which are placed upon us by jobs, family and society. We are likely to periodically experience flu-like symptoms: muscle aches, headaches, feeling intense heat and cold within our bodies, non-specific aches and pains, sinusitis, congestion and feelings of toxicity. Sudden shooting pains in the head and eyes, ringing in the ears, mood swings are all symptoms of our bodies trying to constantly adjust to the energy. The energies are sent up and down the spine and distributed into the body through currently known energy pathways. If one of our pathways is weak, we will feel the symptoms of this organ of the body failing. Our skin may react by stinging, prickling or burning, as we experience circulation restriction and increased flow alternately. This increased change in the amount and type of energy moving through the head and into the body may also cause brain swelling. It is important to see someone who does Cranio sacral adjustments. If the plates of the skull are allowed to become rigid, headaches will occur. If the sutures between the bones of the skull are loosened through Cranial sacral adjustments, the brain can expand and contract without causing pain. When we experience any of these symptoms it may become necessary for us to seek the assistance from competent energy balancers. There are many systems and methods which have been given by Spirit to assist us with these energy transitions. Once we begin to transmute our own energies and systems, we will be used to transmute a portion of the energies for the collective. As willing participants we have, prior to incarnation, agreed to serve as vessels of transmutation.

This process may be VERY difficult for us physically, emotionally and psychologically. We may feel we have dealt with a situation only to find it reoccurring in our lives. It is important to remember that we are doing it for the collective. This is a time when systems such as the <u>CELLULAR RELEASE PROCESS</u> would help - the CD is available from Namaste Enrichment Center. Each of us, because of our uniqueness and the uniqueness of the assignments that we agreed to, which we often do not remember, will be processing for different parts of the collective. We must honor our uniqueness. DISCERNMENT IS EXTREMELY IMPORTANT! When medical assistance is required, seek it. Medicine is as much a miracle as organic measures. Many times it is totally necessary and appropriate to seek medical intervention. Fortunately, there are some physicians now available who recognize there is an energy shift taking place. Ask around to find a physician in your area who is aware and competent to assist you.

Many people are experiencing interfering energies. It is important to recognize that possession and interference by disembodied astral entities does exist, especially now that we are in the midst of the Fourth dimension, which has previously been known by Christians as hell. We are living in a dimension previously only inhabited by beings that were without physical bodies and with not enough energy to make it into the Light, or what we think of as the Fifth dimension which is what Christians think of as Heaven. You have the authority to call upon the Archangel Michael and the Band of Mercy to take any invading energies and entities into the Light so that they may continue to grow and prosper and to not continue to interfere with evolution.

Extreme doubt, fear, addictions and mental and emotional confusion are symptomatic of interference by astral energies. These entities encourage conflict, fear, anger, and increased sexual energies, because these are the energies they need in order to continue to exist. They are particularly attracted to persons who are weak or already addicted to some substance or behavior. They are dead and cannot feed their addiction without attaching themselves to the body of someone who is practicing their drug or behavior of choice. If you believe you or someone you know is suffering from possession or periodic interference from astral entities, call forth the Archangel Michael and the Band of Mercy; but never get into a direct conflict with a possessing or interfering entity. Use the **Prayer of Exorcism** you'll find on a previous page.

Emotionally and psychologically, many of us are experiencing alternating symptoms of density and sudden feelings of lightness in our bodies and emotions; manic-depressive symptoms; feelings of bloatedness, no matter what we eat. Mentally, sometimes in the middle of a sentence, we forget what we were trying to express. We seem to be experiencing memory loss. As we change, it becomes more difficult to reference the past. In fact, all useless data is being erased from our memories. We are being forced energetically to operate only in the NOW. Our past reality was based on our beliefs and our experiences. As these are being erased, we are forced to base our reality on what we "know" in the moment.

If we focus our energies on what is dying, we only prolong the inevitable and increase the chaos. Our souls presume we are concentrating on what we desire. **The Universe increases that which is given mental and emotional energy by us.** It is time to take our eyes off the drama and the chaos and to turn within, where the answers lie. When we listen within, we know what is "ours to do." We cease to feel overwhelmed by the collective chaos. Each of us has a specific part to play in the creation and the solving of the problems we have created for Earth. No one group or person can solve the problems we have collectively created. It is time to hold a collective vision. It is time for us to concentrate not on the problems, but on the solutions, to concentrate on how we desire life on Earth to be.

When we do this the Universe then have an image of what we wish to see created and energized.

If we listen to the voice of the media, we see chaos in World affairs, disputes, killing, war and violence. We are creatures who wish to be able to have World interest, World involvement, and peace of mind, prosperity and comfortable lives simultaneously. This is only possible if we begin and end by listening within. We are multi-dimensional beings. We must listen to all of our selves. It is important to mentally form a committee of our ego, our inner child, our Spirit and all levels of our Oversouls and to get a report from all our selves, before we, as Chairman of the Board, make all of our daily decisions of action. If we listen to the media, we cannot solve our situation, either personally or collectively. The media is invested in keeping us in a state of fear and need. Our bodies and minds need periods of silence from the overabundance of stimulation. Physical exercise is extremely helpful, especially stretching movements such as yoga and dance.

It is recommended by Spirit that we do not ask to hear or see our answers, but that we ask to know. By asking our souls the question: WHAT IS THE NEXT SINGLE THING FOR ME TO DO OR KNOW FOR ME TO BE IN A STATE OF DIVINE GRACE? We will receive an answer. If we turn within and expect to have the answers, we will know what is "ours to do." We may not hear an actual voice, but we can begin by trusting our intuition. Seeing spiritually is possible in the Third and Fourth dimension, spiritual hearing is possible in the fourth and lowest part of the Fifth dimension. Most of us who are awake spiritually now came from higher than the Fifth dimension where the means of communication is knowingness. Ask your soul for knowingness. With knowingness, energetically we will know which of the pieces of information we are exposed to is ours to retain, and we will know which is ours to pass on. We will know what to avoid, and we will know what to let pass us by as unworthy of our time, or "not ours to do." We can then rest in the peace that at any given time we can turn within and "know" what to do in any given situation, whether that situation be a job change, where to live or with whom to have a relationship. If we pay attention to our intuition, it will also let us know what movies to see, what TV programs to watch, what books to read, what to read in the newspapers, and what periodicals to take. We can begin to trust that we will always know all that we need to know, at any given time. We can give up concern about what parts of the Earth are going to survive the changes. Where will be the safe places to live? How much food should we store, etc? We can truly trust that at the time we need to know, we will know everything we need to know in order to fulfill our part of the Plan. No one "makes" us, we "make" ourselves.

We need not fear others, because what they say or think about us can only hurt if we do not have the security of knowing, within ourselves, who we are and what we choose to be. When we choose to be responsible for ourselves, peace will reign within us. Peace is a conscious choice. Peace is the absence of fear. We must be responsible for our own creations, what lies in our own individual Worlds. When we each choose peace, then and only then will there be peace on Earth. We are in control of evolution. We are not here merely to survive. We are here to evolve. We contain the seeds of the new civilization, the new species. One of our greatest hindrances to becoming all we are created to be is for us to be empathic.

## 39.

# How To Transcend Being Empathic To Become Consciously Multi-Dimensional

Do you have trouble focusing? Trouble losing weight? Have headaches the doctors can't explain? Feel crazy occasionally? Get so emotional you can't function without an obvious reason? You may be suffering from being empathic.

At birth we have a tendency to be energetically like little amoebas. We have unstructured borders to our energy fields. We move our energy fields in and around the energy fields of other people in order to check out how they are feeling. We do this instinctively in order to know how to get what we want, in order to be safe, or to comprehend that which is around us. We become "empathic."

To be "empathic" is to consciously or unconsciously project oneself into the consciousness of another Human being, at the emotional or energetic level, in order to have sympathetic or empathic understanding of the other Human being.

As we grow older, some people learn other methods of defense, verbal understanding or soul communication in order to get the needed information. Many people remain empathic, never knowing if the pains and emotions in their bodies are theirs or belong to the people they have encountered. They remain ignorant that they are even picking up feelings and emotions from others and believe that all this confusion and turmoil is their own.

We are never in control of our own feelings as long as we continue to be either consciously or unconsciously empathic. An empathic person finds it very difficult to understand where they stop and other people begin. They have a tendency to allow their boundaries to be invaded by other people.

They do not even understand the concept of personal boundaries. When a person is unconsciously empathic, it is difficult for them to have a good self-image. Their self-image is controlled by the thoughts other people have about them. They do not have a clear impression of selfhood and "others". When a person is unconsciously empathic, the gift of being able to read other people empathically becomes more of a curse than a gift.

When I meet a psychic person who is reading others by being empathic, they are often resistant to the idea of giving up being empathic, believing this is their "gift" and that they must remain empathic in order to fulfill their destiny. If they are willing to trust their souls, they can reprogram themselves to receive necessary information about their clients by being consciously multi-dimensional rather than empathic. It does, however, take discipline to change our way of being energetically. When I use the word discipline many people hear the word punishment. To be disciplined is to care enough about yourself to do what is to your highest good; it is a form of self-love, self-respect.

When a person is empathic they respond emotionally, usually with tears, when large amounts of spiritual energy enter their bodies during readings or meditations. This causes discomfort for them and for their client and is not necessary.

Being empathic is against Spiritual Law, is intrusive and self-sabotaging. In being empathic, we are picking up information from others and carrying it for them, or acting it out for them, unconsciously. It is difficult to differentiate between what are our feelings and emotions and the emotions of others. If you have been consciously or unconsciously empathic, it is time to give up this means of accessing information about others.

Being empathic causes many people to be overweight, excessively emotional or to become addicted to substances, because of being overly sensitive. When the body has no boundaries to the emotional body, the physical body tries to become the size of the emotional body. This feeling of being out of control emotionally leads to excessive eating in order to try to feel in control or to feel grounded. We erroneously try to create a physical barrier between ourselves and other people, since we have no emotional boundary.

It is also possible, when we are not in control of our energy bodies, to attract astral plane entities that want to feed off of our excess emotional energy. Entities who die in a state of addiction cannot feed their addiction once they no longer have physical bodies. They will seek to join the body of someone who is practicing their behavior of choice, whether that be overeating, smoking or using drugs, sex or alcohol in order to feel in their bodies or in order to feel grounded.

If you are concerned that you have entities attached to you or someone you know, never try to confront an astral entity. You have the power to exorcise these energies or entities by using the **PRAYER OF EXORCISM** on page 79.

If we choose to act responsibly energetically, it is time for us to give up being empathic in favor of being deliberately multi-dimensional. To do this, we have to rewrite our software to only seek Oversoul communication with our own Oversoul and to deliberately program ourselves to communicate with others from our Oversoul to their Oversoul. This form of communication bypasses the emotional body. When we need information about another person we can communicate with our Oversouls, and if it is ours to know, our Oversoul will communicate with the Oversoul of the other person and the information or awareness we need will come into us in the form of intuition or knowingness.

If we agree to communicate in this way, after our soul disconnects from the other person's soul, we are not left with any feelings, diseases or emotions that rightfully belong to the other person. In this form of communication we also bypass what is called the morphonogenic field of thought that has built up over time between us and people with whom we are familiar. This field operates like a rut that develops over a period of time between people who communicate often, such as spouses, lovers, children or parents. When one person speaks to the other, the energy of information goes through the rut and the responsive party already believes they know what the speaker is going to say. They "hear" it in the way they have always heard as warped by the rut. If we go directly to our soul to communicate with their soul, the words we speak will have a different energy and we may be actually "heard" for the first time. Their soul gives us intuitive awareness of analogies and verbiage that will gain their attention.

The body is a bio-magnetic computer system for the soul. It can be reprogrammed with new software. The new software is installed by intention. We can cease to be unconsciously empathic by deliberately grounding ourselves each morning by installing intentional balloons or cushions of energy around ourselves, and by having an intention to communicate telepathically or through direct knowingness (rather than empathically) with the Oversouls of those we encounter.

The more open we become energetically, the more information we will pick up from our environment and each other. In order to avoid picking up information unintentionally, it is useful to practice the following grounding exercise to reprogram our body, mind and Spirit. If we change our method of communication we can choose to pick up information only when that is our intention rather than randomly.

# 40.

# Grounding Exercise

This exercise will take approximately two minutes each morning. If you catch yourself behaving empathically during the day, stop and redo the process.

*In a standing position, take a deep breath and focus on the soles of your feet. As you exhale, deliberately intention beams of energy about the size of fluorescent light bulbs (or Luke Skywalker's light saber) going from the soles of your feet into the central core energy of the Mother Earth. (Or see yourself as a tree with roots going into the center of the Earth.)*

*Take another deep breath and as you exhale, focus on your heart, deliberately opening your heart in love and appreciation to the Earth, to your physical body, and* **to** *your Oversoul (God, the sky, the Universal Life Force Energy, or whatever vision works for you.)*

*Take another deep breath and as you exhale open the crown of your head and deliberately send a beam of energy, about the size of a fluorescent light tube into the Cosmic Christ Consciousness level of your own Oversoul. (Send the beam of energy to the Sun or to God, or whatever image works for you.)*

*Continuing to breathe deeply, begin to swing your arms gently at your sides to and fro, back and front, as if you are pumping energy up from the Earth. When you feel the energy begin to flow, change your focus to above your head and begin to pump energy down from your Oversoul. As you pump, you want to also intention pumping up balloons of energy around your body. The first balloon is white and is about 12 feet in all directions from the body; the second balloon, which is pink and inside the first, is about 8 feet in all directions from the body. The third balloon is purple and is about four feet in all directions from the body. The purple balloon becomes your personal energy supply, impenetrable by others. The white and pink energy* fields are excess energy, which you can afford to share with others. Very few people on the planet are spiritually adept enough to penetrate your personal energy field if you use this system.

This process will take about two minutes each morning and begins to create a cocoon or barrier of protection between yourself and other people and other dimensions, other than the information coming directly to you from your soul. It removes the static. It also protects you from astral plane interference and possible possession by astral entities.

Joy, love and hope are energies we have the authority to call forth from the Universe for ourselves and for Earth. There is great power in joy. Miracles are created by the energies of joy.

**What we focus on mentally and emotionally increases or expands.**

Our souls take our thoughts and emotions literally. The soul always believes we are focusing on what we desire. If we focus on debt, it is assumed by the soul that we desire more debt. If we focus on fear, the soul believes we desire more fear. If we focus on illness, the soul believes we desire more illness. If we are lonely, the soul assumes we wish to remain lonely. Stop spending time and energy worrying. Spend your time focusing only on what you desire for yourself, your family and the World. Do not use the words "want and need" or the soul will believe you wish to continue wanting or needing. Use I now desire, intend and gratefully accept.

If finding the purpose for your whole life seems to be too much to decide, then decide the purpose for this one day or simply the next hour. If you still feel stuck, try: "My purpose in life is to cooperate with my Creator."

Don't make the mistake of saying, later when I figure out what my real, ultimate purpose is, then I'll start living my life.

START NOW!!!

Write what you **know** and **act** on it. You will learn all you need in the process. Your higher purpose will unfold before you as you progress through life. It is not necessary to visualize your desires, but it is important to be able to imagine having the life that includes your heart's desires.

# 41.

# The Mystery Of Imagination

Textbooks and dictionaries seem unable to agree on any definition of imagination. The thesaurus lists over 50 synonyms. But, since all of us have imagination, each of us has first-hand knowledge of what it is and does. It seems to me there are two kinds of imagination: creative and non-creative. One runs itself, which is non-creative and includes uncontrollable and unhealthy forms such as hallucinations, delusions of grandeur, persecution complexes, inferiority complexes, martyr complexes, nightmares, fears, imagining hurts to one's feelings, hypochondria, enjoying imaginary ills and obsessive worry. These all involve the desire to run away from difficulty—to misuse one's imagination as a way to flee from reality. The other form, creative imagination, we can control and drive.

Worry is a non-creative form of imagination, all too normal and too often accepted as uncontrollable. We can change worry by substituting positive and constructive pictures of life, its meaning and its possibilities for destructive and fearful imaginings. Imagination is an integral part of the Human mind-body function. Never underestimate the value of ideas. Make an effort to think up a new idea every day. Doing this increases your mental acuity. Think of making imagination your hobby. Creative power can be stepped up by effort and there are ways to improve our creative thinking.

Learning institutions have slighted development of the Human creative mind in favor of filling the student's mind with facts to memorize and remember. The thinking mind is a Human's greatest gift. We have two minds; the judicial mind, which analyzes compares and chooses; and the creative mind, which visualizes, foresees and generates ideas. Judgment has its place and keeps imagination on track. Imagination not only opens ways to action, but also can enlighten judgment.

Most of Humanity ignores their creativity, assigning it to artists and inventors. Only in forced circumstances do many people attempt to try to use their creative minds.

## 42.

# Imagination Is Humanity's Greatest Gift

Without the use of the imagination, Humanity would still be a species living on seeds, fruit, roots and uncooked flesh. The inventing of the wheel, the use of fire, the use of water for power, the harnessing of electricity, the creation of engines, the invention of tools, the vice and the fulcrum, has changed Humanity's life forever. And now the invention of radios, televisions, telephones, microwaves, x-rays, computers, the Internet, email, Face book, twitter, blogs, I-Tunes, LinkedIn, web sites, cell phones, i-Pads, CD's, DVD's, DVR, GPS, satellites, flash drives, etc., has caused us to be a truly global society. It was only about 500 years ago that Europe began to rate the power of thinking, and especially creative thinking, on par with the power of brute force. This new attitude was the essence of the Renaissance.

The invention of the internal combustion engine improved the farming and manufacturing industries to the extent that production put many people out of work. Imagination had to create new industries to create new jobs.

When I think back, even in my lifetime, at all the things that have been invented, I am astonished. It seems that with each generation creative, inventive progress has speeded up. And now, in this Information Age, electronic and digital ideas and inventions are coming so fast and being developed so swiftly as to be mind-boggling. Competition has forced business to recognize the importance of conscious creative effort. Many companies have hired teams of creative researchers to improve their products and their advertising.

Ideas have been, and can be, the solution to almost every Human problem. Ideas are gifted to Humanity from higher vibrational sources. The people who get quiet and listen, pay attention, receive inspiration of new ideas and, if they act on those ideas, they increase their abundance. The word inspiration comes from "to inspire" meaning "to be filled with Spirit." The fact that ideas are sent to the patent office from all over the World and must be stamped with date and time proves that those who listen are receiving these ideas from higher realms and that the ideas are available to anyone. Remember in my story where the woman in Hurst, TX and I both received the message to manufacture greeting cards that were so similar? To receive the solutions to the problems Humans have created for themselves and for the Earth, it will take people who are willing to listen and to implement the ideas that are given down from higher realms.

By spending time listening, whether we do it by meditating or simply paying attention to our thoughts when we are doing repetitive actions, we can be gifted with ideas and inspiration to lift ourselves over the seeming obstacles in our lives. The more ideas we think up or, more accurately, receive the richer and more satisfying our lives are likely to be. Worry is essentially a misuse of imagination. If we use the time and energy we usually spend worrying in imagining creative solutions our lives will be smoother and more enjoyable. The lack of creative effort or the misuse of imagination is often at the core of mental unrest and nervous upsets. Doing something creative will calm the nerves and improve self-esteem and self-respect.

When we don't feel well, we can cause ourselves to feel better by thinking of something worthwhile. A sense of well-being flows from having an idea and putting it into words or actions. The more we attempt to create, the better we will feel. Creative work can be fun. No people enjoy their work as much as those who deal with ideas. We can get more fun out of life by making more use of our imaginations. The more creative we are, the more we will feel fulfilled as a people.

All of us have within us some Divine creative urge. Everyone has hunches. Everyone has intuition. Everyone has the ability to receive inspiration from higher dimensions. The more we intend to receive inspiration and creative ideas the more we will receive them. It takes practice to shut out negative thinking and worry and transform those habits of thought into listening to our intuition for ideas and inspiration and then it takes courage and action to follow through with implementing the ideas we are given.

We have all been given creative talents. The degree of our talent is largely influenced by effort. It is often our drive, rather than the degree of talent, that determines our creative ability. Actual doing is the best exercise of our creative ability. The way to create is to create, just as the way to write is to write. It is a proven fact that during war time people make more effort to be creative. When the need arises, Humans, by nature, begin to be more creative. Our imaginations seem to work harder when driven by duty, desperation, need or affection.

There is no evidence that higher education induces creative power. For one thing, most educational institutions ignore the subject of imagination. In America, supposedly due to lack of funding, the public schools are closing out the creative arts programs of art, drama and music and keeping reading, writing, math and science. Many highly educated persons are sterile creatively, while others accomplish outstanding results in spite of almost total lack of formal instruction.

Creative power sometimes makes up for lack of technical schooling or specialized training. The telegraph was worked out by Morse, a professional painter of portraits. The steamboat was thought up by Fulton, also an artist. Eli Whitney was a school teacher who devised the cotton gin. Irving Berlin had no musical training. It was said of him, "He can neither read music nor transcribe it – he can only give birth to it." Ford and Edison both lacked formal education.

Higher education gives us a greater grasp on life, a more orderly way of thinking, clearer judgment. These gains are useful to good living, but the extent of one's creative power does not depend upon a degree. Self-confidence is one of the keys to increased creativity. Imagination lasts longer than memory. We can keep our creative power, regardless of age, as long as we keep our desire. Our creative ability can keep growing year after year in pace with the effort we put into it. Imagination grows by exercise. Imagination is like muscle, if we don't use it, it will atrophy. Although older people have a tendency to lose some of their memory power, creative imagination is ageless. To write fiction takes more creative power than writing fact.

If we allow ourselves to get in a rut, quit being curious and just stop trying, we cannot help but be less creative. Ideas often come when we are bathing, shaving, putting on makeup, driving, taking a walk, folding laundry, gardening, riding a bike, exercising, meditating, sewing, riding a bus, a train, an airplane, doing routine or repetitive actions. Often the best ideas come when we are falling asleep or just as we wake up. At these times our brain frequency has slowed and we are in an alpha state of consciousness, receptive to receiving higher vibrations of thought from other dimensions. We are more likely to be operating from our right brain.

Insomnia is often a sign that our soul is attempting to communicate with us. Insomnia may awaken creativity. If we fear we will not be able to sleep and worry over our wakefulness, we are more likely not to be able to fall asleep or stay asleep. If we make it a practice to pick something to think about for which we want ideas, we can use the time of wakefulness more positively and usually our creativity will reward us with insights and ideas. Remember, don't be mad that you are having trouble falling asleep; instead, seek something creative to think over. If you awaken in the middle of the night and have trouble going back to sleep, rather than worry about not sleeping or worry about some situation in your life, invite your soul to give you creative inspiration. Sit up with pencil and pad and listen. Spirit muses love the middle of the night and early morning when most activity and sound have ceased around us. When there is the least amount of activity and static in the ethers it is easier to receive creative, inspired ideas. Do not use the time to fret. Utilize the time to write or to read something useful, which will usually cause you to fall asleep.

A good long shower or bath will cleanse the aura of thought forms and emotions and clear the way for sleep, meditation or increase mental clarity for receiving creative inspiration. Chores are also good coaxers of creative ideas because most chores are repetitious, such as weeding, mowing the lawn, mopping, vacuuming, folding laundry, reorganizing a cabinet or drawer, ironing, doing dishes or emptying the dishwasher.

Many of us travel to and from work. Travel time can be used creatively if we don't distract ourselves with radio, newspaper, emailing, playing computer games, and reading or have music going. Silence is helpful, but not essential to receiving inspired ideas. If you are driving, having a recorder in your pocket or console is useful. If you take a bus, train, plane or subway the vibrations and rhythm of the vehicle can inspire ideas. Writing thoughts can be useful even if you only carry 3 by 5 cards on which to capture ideas. I've found I'm more creative when writing by hand than typing into a computer or electronic device. There is something about the hand moving a pencil across paper that connects to the creative part of my brain. When I first started receiving information from my soul I wrote with number two graphite pencils. The organic substances of wood and graphite seem conducive to allowing the energy to flow through me and onto the paper. Do not try to edit what you receive until a later time.

Concentration is important. Concentration is nothing but attention sharply focused and steadily sustained and is an acquired habit rather than a natural gift. It does take effort, but with practice it is possible to focus one's attention even in a noisy or busy situation. Fatigue and apathy do more to kill concentration than noise or crowds.

We have reproductive imagination, which makes it possible for us to bring pictures back into our minds of things previously seen. We also have the ability to have controlled or structured visualization, which includes deliberately creating a vision of a desired object or objective. We have a vicarious imagination, which makes it possible to feel for others. People go to theatres, watch movies and soap operas mainly to lose themselves in the lives of others. We do the same thing when reading, but reading is less passive in terms of the effort it requires to mentally construct the scenes and actions.

The Golden Rule embodies the noblest use of vicarious imagination. To "do unto others," we have to imagine how they would like to be treated, as well as know how we would like to be treated. This also holds true for choosing gifts for others.

Anticipative imagination makes it possible for us to think ahead, makes it possible for us to guess. Anticipative imagination can be used to deliberately brighten each day. We can look forward to our most pleasant part of the day ahead. We can imagine everything going our way. We can imagine positive exceptions being made in our favor. The highest form of anticipative imagination is creative expectancy. When we look forward to something we want to come true, and strongly believe that it will come true, we can often make ourselves make it come true.

Creative imagination involves hunting and changing what is found. Hunting and changing are the two powers that enable a creative thinker to arrive at new ideas. We can find something that is not really new, but is new to us. There is a difference between discovery and invention. We can discover something, as Newton did gravity and as Franklin did electricity, but the inventive imagination comes into play when the discoverer chooses to use the discovery in a creative manner. Think of all the ways the association of ideas has used both of these discoveries. A person can discover that light can also be used for heat. Imagination can bring together those things or thoughts which are not new in and of themselves, but can be cooked up into that which is new. This happens every day, especially in the creation of new recipes.

Creativity is more than mere imagination. It is imagination inseparably coupled with both intent and effort. Creative imagination may be thought of as the action of mind which produces a new idea or insight. What sparks the spark? We have not yet learned what makes the heartbeat. Creative imagination is just as mystic or more so. It is evidence of divinity. There is at work in the World an influence which may be described as creative. It is capable of reinforcing life and enhancing natural faculty

Creativity requires forward thinking. Creative imagination uses the material of previous experience to produce something new rather than reproducing the past. The knowledge and experiences we have tucked away in our mind are indispensable. Imagination, like reason, cannot run without the fuel of knowledge, but constant awareness is essential. First-hand experience provides the richest fuel for creative power. Second-hand experience—such as reading, listening or spectating—gives us far thinner fuel. Prosperity often tends to impoverish us creatively, whereas hard going or struggle tends to call forth our creativity. Travel is another rich source of creative inspiration.

Remaining alert and continuing our self-education steps up our creative power. Self-education causes us to observe as many worthwhile facts as possible. It is important to remember what we have observed and to combine the facts to come to creative conclusions. The effort we put into self-education pays off in added creative power.

In observing today's children, I wonder if we are doing them a disservice. Most of the things they are exposed to "murder wonder." Most children are not exposed in creative ways to nature. For the most part their play, sports and education are so regimented as to remove curiosity and wonder.

Association plays a big part in the accidental factor of creativity. The association of ideas is what gears imagination to memory and causes one thought to lead to another. The ancient Greeks stated as the three Laws of Association: contiguity, similarity, and contrast. By contiguity they meant nearness, as when a baby's shoe reminds you of an infant. By similarity they meant that a picture of a lion will remind you of your cat. By contrast they meant that a midget might remind you of a giant. There is also the Law of Cause and Effect, which means that a yawn may remind you it is time to retire. Association can be enriched by selective attention. Association can also work through sounds or smells rather than words. Smells can evoke chains of thought and are one of our strongest forms of remembered associations.

Our power of association will produce more ideas if we keep a notebook and jot down our hunches, our observations and our conclusions. Ideas are flighty things and are often as hard to remember as our dreams. Although many of your ideas may not work out, there is a good chance they may suggest other thoughts. I keep 3 by 5 cards beside where I read and keep a small notebook in my purse and a recorder in my car for this purpose. Checklists, note pads, purposely being positive, stick-to-it-tiveness can all cause our power of association to well up more ideas for us out of the storage in our memory.

Many people believe that combination is the essence of creativity, that a creative thinker evolves no new ideas; they actually evolve new combinations of ideas which are already in their mind. One of the richest men in Oklahoma saw a box sitting atop a folding chair. His mind took the image farther and put wheels on the chair and invented the grocery cart. As a child, Pasteur had a memory of neighbors being poisoned and driven crazy by bites from a rabid wolf. Pasteur created many man-guarding vaccines, but he was most driven to find a vaccine to cure the victims of rabies because of the dreadful childhood memory.

Creative thinking is not purely an intellectual process; the thinker is dominated by their emotions and their will. Emotional drive is self-starting and largely automatic, whether based on hunger, fear, love or ambition. The other kind of energy depends upon determination rather than feelings, and has to be cranked.

Every brain has a section that can create ideas. It is called the "silent area" since it controls no body-movement and has nothing to do with what we see or hear or physically feel. It is a lump of tissue called the thalamus. In this area of the brain, our basic emotions are centered. It is known that ideas flow faster under emotional stress. When in a jam our imaginations often soar. The emotional part is wired by nerves to the frontal area in such a way as to affect creative thinking.

Fright is too treacherous a drive, because it is an animal urge that throws us back to where we were before our intellects developed. Fright is akin to fear of punishment. Fear of punishment may make us work hard physically, but a person cannot focus their creative mind when obsessed by fear of punishment. Even the slightest degree of coercion tends to cramp imagination. Dictators and totalitarian rulers work hard to keep fear alive in the people they rule. They are aware that freedom will cause creative thinking and revolt.

Love and patriotism are better driving powers. Love of country inspired hundreds of thousands of our people to think up ideas that helped to win the first and second World Wars. Hard going induces hard effort in the nation as well as in the individual. Creative effort in times of prosperity has tended to ebb, whereas depressions have brought about extra efforts that have resulted in much advancement.

Love makes the average woman unceasingly think up things for her family. Maternal drive generates far more ingenious effort than thirst, hunger or sex. Love when turned to hate can lift a non-creative person to creative heights. Many criminals are highly creative, but choose to use their creativity in non-productive ways.

Fear of poverty is an even stronger urge than the hope for wealth. The spirit of intellectual adventure, vanity, and the desire for self-realization can be motivators. Lack of childhood security fuels some people to excel. It has spurred me into a habit of effort I don't think I would possess if I had been raised with a sense of security. Being raised in lower economic circumstances caused me to develop a habit of creative effort, making something better from what was available in front of me. I acquired a master's degree in "making do." I've never been particularly motivated by deadlines, but deadlines put some people into a hyper creative mode.

Some people can start themselves thinking creatively by asking themselves questions: "What can I do to get ahead in my job? What can I do to make this party, this relationship a success?"

Most people fear attempting to be creative because of fear of judgment, their own and the fear of their creation being judged by others. Creative thinking calls for a hopeful, positive, enthusiastic attitude, which can be easily quashed by the critical judgment of others. It is good to not let anyone read, see or be aware of your creativity until you have completed it to your own satisfaction. Premature judgment can stop the flow of creativity. It is important to not let our own inner critic sap our creative ideas and efforts. We need self-encouragement to be creative. We also need to be self-disciplined in order to not abandon our own ingenuity. Our need to conform often stifles our creativity. Praise tends to make creativity bloom, while judgment, discouragement, wisecracks and criticism kills it.

Perfectionism kills creativity. Many artists are jealous and many art teachers are not supportive of young talent, because they fear being out done. Be careful in choosing a teacher who is strong enough in their own creativity to not be threatened by the talent of others. Choose teachers who are encouraging and supportive. Often we did not have a choice in teachers while we were in school and teachers have the power to demolish a person's self-confidence in their creative ability. I let myself be stopped artistically in the third grade and didn't begin again until after I was forty due to the judgment of one teacher. Everyone needs encouragement to be creative.

Creative people succeed because they begin, they try, they attempt, they experiment, and they just keep trying. Too many people fear even attempting to be creative by comparing themselves to others they feel are extremely gifted creatively. We never know what we are capable of creatively until we attempt and don't give up after the first attempt but stick to it and discipline ourselves to show up regularly with materials that can spark creativity. The trouble with the average person is that they do not sufficiently trust themselves to create and to deliver ideas. The more creative thinking and action we do, and the more ideas we express, the more competent we become, and with creative effort comes a most satisfying sense of accomplishment.

**Make the goal of cherishing your experience more important than the goal of getting somewhere.**

**Spirituality and creativity exist in different dimensions than ordinary time.**

Whatever it is you desire, you must become this in your mind, words, feelings, desires, and actions. Act as if, and you are. The outer must correspond to the inner.

There are two kinds of action: required action and inspired action. Required action would be to gain the necessary education and internship if you desire to be a doctor. Inspired action, on the other hand, comes from inner spiritual urges that spark one's passion such that one wants to take immediate action on them.

Often when we begin to practice the art of manifestation, or anything else, we will reach a plateau where it seems as if nothing else is happening. This plateau often causes people to quit or give up, but if we continue to practice we find that life happens in peaks and valleys. You never know how your practice/efforts/actions will produce results. Anyone can commit to do anything for a minute. Life is only lived one minute at a time. Mastering anything requires patience.

Do whatever you are doing 100 percent, regardless of how small or insignificant it may seem at the time. Give it your best.

Experience a sense of joy in whatever your present activity, regardless of how mundane. Notice the sensual feel of what's on your hands when you wash dishes or the fresh smell of clean sheets as you make your bed or fold the laundry. By paying attention to the colors, the textures and sounds, the tastes, and the smells, you experience present moment connectedness with everything. This attention heightens your awareness of being present and enriches your life. The core work of living a Humanly successful and divinely spiritual life is to stay present no matter what you are doing.

**It is not what we teach that is most learned—it is what we are.**

It is far easier to teach Truth than to practice It, but the practice is the teaching. We are surrounded by an all-pervasive Spirit of God. That Spirit is the creator of life and the World and that Spirit is within us.

We may not feel we are in control of all the events of our lives, but we are or can be in control of how we respond to them. Learning to choose our responses to outer events and merging our will of self with the will of God is the ultimate goal to a happy and successful life.

When we learn to trust our instincts, our intuition, and the multidimensional timing of things, we step into lives that are more expansive and sweeter than anything we have imagined. I often say, "Thy will be done" and follow it by, "But could you hurry?"

I've found that Spirit's attention and the feeling of being loved, heard and cherished by my soul has fulfilled much of my longing to have these things from other people.

**The only thing that matters is following your truth.**

Make the goal of cherishing your experience more important than the goal of getting somewhere. Practice allowing yourself to do what you can do, when you can do it. If you didn't do something yesterday, do it today. If you can't do it right now, do it in an hour. If you can't do all of it, do some of it.

If I choose, there is nothing in my thoughts about the past that can in any way deny me the pleasure and privilege of living today as though everything was complete and perfect.

**When I focus on my expectation, instead of what IS happening, I miss the opportunity to be happy.**

The culture of constant productivity actually makes us less productive, because it distracts us from our surroundings and the sense of oneness we can experience when we pay attention to where we are. It heightens our anxiety, because there is always one new message to be answered, one new thing to do.

Practicing a Namaste attitude, acknowledging the spirit within you and the spirit within others and by approaching people with compassion and an awareness of their divinity can be a challenging but transformative spiritual practice.

# 43.
# Attracting The Life We Desire

All things are constructed of atoms, from our bodies to the Solar System. You can call it magnetism, polarity, electricity, moving intelligence or God. It is everywhere. The thing that causes this energy to take physical form is thought. By changing our thoughts and beliefs, we can set up an entirely new field of magnetism within and around our bodies to attract those things we have been repelling previously by fear, limited thoughts or negative thinking.

Our Conscious Mind is the master. Our Sub-conscious Mind is the servant; it takes what we think and believe, literally, and creates it in our lives. Even if we say things in jest such as, "I feel like I've been run over by a truck" or something like "that breaks my heart," we are inviting disaster because our Sub-conscious Mind will quickly make an effort to create what we have described.

The Conscious Mind has compartments of memory, reason and imagination. The Conscious Mind exists at the level of the five senses and is quite logically a product of hearing, seeing, smelling, feeling and tasting. Its pursuit is to satisfy each of these five senses with sensations that provide pleasure instead of pain. The Conscious Mind is a pleasure and pain distinguisher and its compartment of memory, reason and imagination are but names given to its total instinct to find pleasure and avoid pain. We are endowed with the life urge to survive.

The Conscious Mind is a recorder, an analyzer and a filer. It records sensation at a level of pain and pleasure; it analyzes this sensation according to circumstances which caused it; and it files such sensation away under one of two main compartments headed "Recall about Pain" and "Recall about Pleasure." Of itself, the Conscious Mind has no memory. In other words, it does not contain a storehouse other than what is connected to experience and sensation. The faculty of memory as applied to the Conscious Mind is simply its ability to recall certain experiences that have been recorded in the Sub-conscious Mind. If we want to remember something for easy recall, it is useful to intend it to be remembered in the short term memory of the Conscious Mind, to verbally suggest to yourself at the time that you intend to remember.

The memory of the Sub-conscious Mind is perfect. Every thought of the Conscious Mind has been indelibly recorded in the Sub-conscious as well as every sensory perception of the individual. The great mass of this material is forever lost to the recall of the Conscious Mind, for it can only be so recalled when it has previously been filed away with instructions to the Sub-conscious Mind to release it for recall. Most of it is not available to our recall.

We have within our Sub-conscious Minds, many stored thoughts and beliefs that we have accepted from mass consciousness and from what we have been taught. Much of what is in our sub-conscious is not true and no longer serves us to our highest good. The only way to reverse a negative belief or thought form is by replacing it with truth, by affirming what is true and what we do desire to believe and attract.

We create ourselves anew in every moment. This allows us to decide what type of person we want to be and make the appropriate choices. Circumstances don't determine who we are and what we become. We do. Each of us creates ourselves however we want. Regardless of what well-meaning authority figures may have told us, we can be, do or have whatever we can conceive and intend. We always have the ability to shape who we are and how we show up.

We are designed to be powerful. We can only use this unique power when we embrace the Spirit within us. Without our connection to that inner power, no amount of worldly power can make a difference. With it, it is the only thing that can, not only make us feel secure or powerful, but also make us feel peaceful. There is no lasting security in machines, electricity, electronics, atomic power or money that is equal to the security one feels when they are consciously connected to their soul, their Source.

We are Spirit. We are the essence of the mighty intelligence that guides and controls the Universe. This intelligence is ours to use as we see fit. It is God-given, a divine birthright and is denied to no Human unless it is ignored and refused. There is only one mover in all creation and that mover is thought. There is only one Creator and that Creator is the Universal Super-conscious Mind, or God. This Superconscious Mind creates for us exactly what we think and believe.

There is cause, there is reason, there is a power greater than we are of which we are a part. We can use this power to a make our lives good or we can ignore it and attempt to use our own power and struggle.

We are born free. Every Human is born free to discover our destiny, free to discover the Source of our being and the immensity of the spiritual power available to each of us. Thought habits of our conscious mind determine our destiny. Most Humans think habitually, repetitiously and without observing what they are thinking.

It is important for us to remember, every day of our lives, the same power that brings good fortune will also bring bad fortune and it does so according to how we use our thoughts. Without control of our thoughts, without witnessing what we are thinking, we create unconscious lives. If we use the power available to us without control, without understanding the Law of Magnetism and the Law of Attraction, and that our Sub-conscious Mind acts literally upon our thoughts we create unconsciously. Our Sub-conscious Mind is the most creative instrument in the Universe; it spans space and time, manifests form from substance, and can reach out to all knowledge. It exists in each of us. It is vitally important what we allow the Conscious Mind to feed into our Sub-conscious Mind.

We have thoughts and ideas in our Sub-conscious Mind planted by our Conscious Mind. They can be referred to as "prompters." These negative prompters have been buried in our Sub-conscious Mind very much like a forgetful dog might bury a bone and not only forget where he buried it, but also that he had buried it. We have thought things, agreed with things that are not true. These things are still buried in our Sub-conscious Minds and we are living our lives from there automatically rather than now affirming the truth and what we do desire to be our current beliefs. They can be things we heard as an infant or a small child such as "There is never enough to go around" or "People cannot be trusted."

A sick person may want to be well, but in their Sub-conscious they harbor phrases such as "there's so much sickness in the World" or "everyone is getting the flu, it's in the air," "there are so many diseases described on the TV now, how can a person be well?"

A lonely person may desire love and friends, yet in their Sub-conscious Mind they repel love by continuing to believe, "people are just out to get what they can out of me. No one can be trusted. I'm not good enough. I'm not attractive enough. I'm not smart enough. Nobody loves me." The Sub-conscious Mind is the great creator and it creates exactly what it is prompted to create whether we remember planting these seeds or not.

We can redo these thoughts, because the Conscious Mind rules the Sub-conscious Mind. Every condition, circumstance and manifestation of our lives can be changed to suit our current conscious desires, but it must be done consciously and with intention and by concentrating on the Spirit within us rather than the desires of the ego. The real us is Spirit; this conscious hidden intelligence that exists behind our eyes is timeless, formless and built from the magnificence of Source. It is not our name, our job, our home or our body; it is the I AM aspect of God.

We are pure Spirit, cast into Human form as a manifestation of Divine Intelligence, existing for a little while on Earth as a Human to fulfill our part of the Divine Plan of God. There is only One Intelligence, One Mind, in all creation and every Human is a part of it. This Universal Mind knows no big or little, rich or poor, great or insignificant. It gives of itself and creates according to our desire and belief.

Think of this Mind, if you will, as a great plastic medium, containing all energy, all knowledge and all substance. Think of it as a medium responsive only to thought and responsive in degree and time according to how our thoughts are charged with desire, belief, expectancy, conviction, gratitude and desire.

**Thoughts plus conviction equals manifestation.**

There is manifested in our experience exactly that which we are convinced is possible. We need not remove all these negative prompters in a special procedure since positive will override negative. All that is necessary is for us to install in the Sub-conscious Mind a group of positive prompters through affirmations fueled by intention.

It is important that we pay close attention to our intuition and to not negate it whether it comes in a dream, repetitive thought, a flash of insight or something someone says to us that is the answer to something we have been questioning. We also need to pay attention to where our faith lies. What do we have faith in? People, money, government or God? Where our faith lies also lies our power to manifest.

Thought is the great creator, master and Mother of the Universe, God in Humans, and the infinite in the immediate. There is no end to individual power through the right use of thought. Our sub-conscious negative prompters act as a closed door to the power of the great Universal Mind in which we live and move and have our being.

The complete removal of all negative prompters in mind, full contact with the Infinite, complete recognition of the Spiritual Laws and the spiritual nature of Humankind is the path provided for us to follow in our journey back to God. Once we admit there is a power greater than us and that we can connect with that power, we can use that power to create healthy, happy, abundant, loving lives. Every physical Law of the Universe has a corresponding Spiritual Law.

Our bodies were created by our souls for their use. Our ego has convinced us to fear and that we are our bodies and the ego has attempted to keep us from knowing ourselves as Spirit inhabiting a Human form. Our bodies are the embodiment of Spirit, aspects of God, for the purpose of expressing God qualities in Human form.

There is a great medium of mind and intelligence that is in and surrounds every Human. This Intelligence is all and knows and does everything. This Intelligence, God, is an eternal Creator, creating that which the minds of Humans think. This invisible plane of Human existence offers the greatest challenge and the greatest hope of Humankind.

**Change the idea of a thing and you change the thing.**

Only you can be you. We are each created uniquely to come to Earth with unique attributes and missions. It does not serve us or our souls to attempt to be like anyone other than ourselves. We are to practice creativity instead of conformity and competition. Our security in life depends entirely on our recognition of our divine nature and contact with our soul.

**We are told that even ten minutes a day spent in meditation affirming our divinity will change our lives for the better quicker than anything else we can do.**

"In the beginning was the word," and it is with all creation, for the word is the thought. Speaking the word with conviction and maintaining that conviction with faith is the complete chain of manifestation from the thought to the thing. Faith is required; faith in God and faith in our own divinity. Make up your mind that the Intelligence that exists behind the Universe does not judge you or destroy Itself. Humankind has created evil and hell. We have Freewill and free choice to create evil, lack, disease and hatred. Or we can obtain good by creating good by the power of our faith and thoughts. God does not punish us. We punish ourselves by disobeying the Law of Karma, the law of Cause and Effect.

There are billions of Conscious Minds thinking into the Universal

Mind, creating physical reality with each thought that is expressed with complete belief. The Universal Mind is reactive, creative and it can create for your neighbor or family what you think into it for them. And it tends to create for you what your neighbor and family thinks into it for you. The Universal Mind acts on the thought behind which there is the most belief and faith.

**Believe you will fail and you will.**
**Believe you will succeed and you will.**

Everything on this Earth is a result of thought. The Universal Mind attempts to manifest all thought to the person thinking it, and it also attempts to manifest it to the entire World. Every thought of every person who has ever lived has been indelibly recorded in Universal Mind which has been moved to action because of it. All thought is not consciously projected into the Creative Mind. Much of what gets expressed by Humans habitually and without deliberate thought becomes expressed. This is why monitoring what we are thinking at all times is so important. Universal Mind recognizes only conception and desire, or thought and emotion, and it recognizes them by creating them into actuality. We are all responsible for our thoughts and beliefs.

Besides Jesus, there have been many enlightened Humans who have lived on this planet. There have been societies of these enlightened Humans whose perception of truth has been so acute that physical manifestation from thought, thought transference and intuition has been common in their daily lives. Yet these Humans and societies have usually thought it dangerous to reveal this knowledge to Humanity as a whole. Jesus taught these same concepts in parables which have been misquoted and mistranslated in order to keep Humans believing we are powerless and sinners.

Through the Law of Attraction, all things come to those who believe in them. The quality of our lives is attracted to us by our beliefs and thoughts. Evil is the result of erroneous thought conception. Erroneous thought conception is the cause of Evil. The Universe is owned and operated by a God of Love. Thoughts of a vengeful God and fear of God has been perpetrated by beings that wish to control others and is not based in truth.

It is important that we quit carrying around the burden of mistakes we believe we have made. It is important that we forgive ourselves and others and to begin to think positively.

We are not alone. We did not create ourselves. We cannot by ourselves do the slightest bit of creating. The power into which we project our thoughts is the only creative force there is. It builds and constructs all form and circumstances, but it does this according to how we think. This power creates what we believe and manifests for us what we can accept. We can create abundance in our experience only if we realize and know that there is abundance all about us and we accept it. In other words, we don't demand money, we don't force money with the idea that there is not enough to go around and we don't have enough of it. We accept money; there is a great abundance of it around us, and we know that. The force of our will against the Universal Mind must inevitably set up the same thing in our experience so that we see opposition instead of cooperation. Have confidence in the power greater than you are and have complete acceptance of good.

The power that creates is the power that knows; and it is possible, with perfect attunement, to achieve in each condition of your life a situation of guidance. When we completely accept the power greater than we are, when we know it will create our experience that which we believe, we will also find that it also will provide us with answers to our questions.

We must let go of our problems once the basic element of the problems are clearly defined in our Conscious Mind, and once our general objective is clearly defined in our Conscious Mind; we must let go. Forget the problem altogether. One morning while we are going about our daily tasks, we will find the solution. It will strike our consciousness with such impact as to remove all doubt it is truth.

There is guidance available. It is not achieved by effort or will. It is achieved by complete acceptance of the power greater than we are that knows the answer. The proper use of Spiritual Law is acceptance and faith. We are to seek balance between our Conscious Mind and our Sub-conscious Mind.

# 44.

# Accept—Believe—Know—Relax— Have Faith

It has only been lately that scientists probing at the elemental substance of nature have yielded us the knowledge that mass and density are purely relative. The astounding discovery of science that there is no such thing as a solid mass has revised the thinking of the World. The only difference between us and what we think of as physical objects is our form of consciousness. There is only one substance from which everything physical is made, there is only one substance from which energy is made and this energy, or substance, is infinite in time and space; it has no beginning and no end and, thus, is everywhere at all times, and all of it is anywhere at any time. There is only one substance or energy or Intelligence in all things. Everything is basically one thing, has no beginning and no end, and has no past and no future, but only one eternal now.

The Sub-conscious Mind reacts entirely by suggestion and has no volition of its own. It does not by itself make choices, indulge in arguments, postulate theories, search for answers, wonder at possibilities. It only accepts and acts on suggestions from the Conscious Mind. It acts on those thoughts behind which there is the most conviction. Once it is given a suggestion, it immediately sets to work to make that suggestion truth, for it accepts that suggestion completely. Intuition is the aspect of mental power which enables a person to contact certain aspects of the Sub-conscious Mind through meditation. The contact comes when we get the Conscious Mind thoughts out of the way. All physical circumstance originates on the plane of thought.

We are to think in terms of complete unity. We are one with every person who lives, ever has lived, every form of life that exists, every inanimate object in our World, because all things are made from one thing. Thus, all things are one thing, and objects and circumstances exist as the result of conception and desire being projected into the infinite creative substance of which we are all a part, in which we are all one.

Thought is the only mover. According to the degree of our conscious intelligence, we will grasp the power that is ours. According to our conscious intelligence, we will project images into the Sub-conscious Mind that we desire to experience. We must consciously exercise control over our thoughts.

The entire Universe is alive. There is nothing dead, nothing inanimate. When Jesus said, "God is not a God of the dead but a God of the living," He was revealing the basic truth of all creation For all is living and all is intelligence and all is conscious; and the great motivating force of all life is its attempt to expand its consciousness. In other words, it seeks to know itself. Evolution is life expanding to a conscious Oneness with God. It is useful to think, "I Am that, I AM."

It can be said that the purpose of life is the attainment of knowledge, the expansion of consciousness, a constant reaching upward and outward and inward toward a Oneness with God. As the Spirit expands its consciousness, it seeks a new form through which to express itself. The body which you now occupy is but an instrument of your consciousness and expression of your knowledge of yourself. By the very nature of your being, your consciousness must grow and, as it does, your Spirit will gradually lay down your current body and return again into the Universal Consciousness where it starts anew in its quest for a new expression. The level we go to when we leave these bodies matches the level of consciousness we have attained in this life.

## 45.

# Becoming A Soul-Infused Personality

A stream of Light connects us to our souls. Some refer to this as the silver cord. It is possible to deliberately increase the size of this cord and to create a bridge into space where we can go for healing or we can invite the etheric body of another to join us on this bridge to create healing in a relationship. This bridge is built through intention. Between our consciousness and the consciousness available from our soul there are magnetic streams of Light. In the back of the neck of the Human species there are seven tensor receptors. These receptors were included in the original matrix of the Homo sapiens. In most Humans I've met, these receptors are not turned on or lit up. When they are dormant it is more difficult to perceive information from our souls. Once we become aware these receptors exist we can activate them through intention during meditation or they can be activated for us by an authorized activator, which I AM. They operate similarly to crystal chips in the original crystal radios we made as children; well, maybe you didn't because you are probably not as old as I AM. We do not have to understand the inside of a radio or television in order to receive information through it. We do need to know how to turn it on and to tune it to the station we desire to pick up. The connections to our soul work in the same way as a radio would pick up transmissions. We do need to be clear what channel, frequency or station we wish to receive. All spiritual growth and manifestation happen through intention. I suggest asking to connect to the highest level of your Oversoul that your physical body can easily tolerate, through the vibration of the Cosmic Christ Consciousness.

I believe it helps to know that these receptors exist in order that we can go into meditation and turn them on. We also have the opportunity to activate three additional chakras in our bodies that will more strongly connect the body with the soul and make it easier for the soul to use the body for the purpose it was created. These three chakras are located as follows: One at the base of the skull is referred to as the "well of dreams chakra"; two is located in the roof of the mouth and is referred to as "the mouth of God chakra," (when activated, this one makes it easier for the soul to speak through the body when it is appropriate); the third is referred to as "the high heart chakra" and is located near the sternum and extends through the body to just below the heart in the back of the body. It corresponds to the opening through which the etheric form leaves the body to have out of body experiences while we are sleeping or can be accomplished through intention when we are meditating. Some people bring spiritual secrets with them from other lifetimes. These secrets are stored in the knees. I am aware when this is true for a client and get down on the floor and tone into the client's knees to break up the capsule of information, which then goes into their blood stream as consciousness.

When we first come to Earth, the silver cord is minimal and enough energy comes from the soul to keep the infant bodies functioning. As the Human body grows, more energy is given from the soul. By the time the Human body is approximately six to seven years old, much of the soul is connected to the body. At this age, many children are able to see into other dimensions and to know things before they happen in this dimension. Most of them, like most of us, were talked out of continuing to "know" or "see" things that others (grownups) did not see or know.

The amount of energy coming to the Earth at this time is tremendous. The process of enlightenment requires a well-integrated personality as a base for our Higher Self to guide us without tremendous resistance from our egos. The amount of Light flowing into our minds can and will stimulate any personality tendency, such as a sense of superiority or inferiority, or an emotion such as sadness, loneliness, grief, jealousy, possessiveness, resentment, the need to control, or anger. Your personality is working very rapidly now to integrate new circuits of reality. Our reality is rapidly changing day by day. If we attempt to live in the World today with the personality we developed twenty years ago, we will be suffering. All of us must spend some time in the presence of people who seem to be stuck in the past. We can observe how afraid or angry this makes them. They do not understand that energy is bombarding them and intensifying their personality traits. To be in public and not get caught up in their fray, it is important to stay connected to our souls, to keep our sense of humor and to remember being in a hurry screws up Divine Timing.

Think of the analogy of us coming to Earth and we are riding in the back seat of a shiny limo. God is driving the limo and we are happy to have the window down between the front and rear seat. At about the age of sixteen, when we get our driver's license, we decide we want to be the driver of our lives and we no longer want to take orders or suggestions from anyone.

Between sixteen and twenty we think we know everything; obviously, we know more than our parents. We put God in the back seat and roll up the window between the front and back and we proceed to make trouble for ourselves. Only when we get lost or desperate do we roll the window down (pray) and ask God to help us out of some mess we have gotten ourselves into. Usually later in life (more so now for many people), we are remembering that we were supposed to be co-creators of our lives. This was supposed to be a joint effort. God sent us down here for a purpose. That purpose involved our continuing to have constant communication with that which sent us. Our purpose is to bring more and higher vibrational energy into this dimension. In an ideal situation we get out of the limo, we invite God to once again take on the driver's seat responsibilities and we get in the back seat or the observers position where we were intended to ride. The intention also is to keep the window down between the front and rear seats; to have a constant communication with God, your soul, or whatever you perceive is who sent you here.

Letting God or your soul be the driver does not in any way mean that you are a pawn and that you are to do everything that is suggested by the soul. You always maintain your Freewill. God or your soul will not override your Freewilll. Suggestions will be made by God or your soul. You are free to consider whether or not you are willing to do what is suggested. If a suggestion seems scary or unclear, it is your responsibility to ask for clarification or to write down conditions under which you would take on the task. If, after you have written down your conditions you begin to see the Universe fulfill your conditions, you are then more obligated to follow through with what the soul has suggested. Some people have accused me of arguing with my soul. I would rather use the term negotiating. In one of the first messages I ever received from Spirit, I was told. "Our will for our life in you will very closely parallel your own true desires, but you must write down your desires. There will always be a way to fulfill your purpose and to enjoy your life."

Most of our problems are created by our ego ruling our personality. If we don't think of ourselves as good enough, pretty enough, strong enough, smart enough, we have a tendency to be inauthentic in our behavior. In each situation, if we continually increase the stream of energy coming into the body from the soul and invite continuous participation from the soul into the personality and the body, our lives will change. At first it may feel awful as each inappropriate personality trait comes to the fore and a circumstance will occur to bring it to our attention. We can choose how to respond now and not just come from reaction. We can become the observer, the designer, the co-creator of a life that fulfills the purpose for which we came to Earth and fulfill our Human desires simultaneously.

An example would be if I receive in meditation that the soul would like the body to be in Santa Fe in two days, I dialog and ask if we can stop in Amarillo along the way and have dinner with a dear friend that lives there and if we can drop down to Lubbock and see my niece and my two grand-nephews on the return to Oklahoma City. I also ask for the perfect place to stay in Santa Fe. After I've written my "suggestions or conditions", it would not be unusual for me to receive a call from someone who is also going to be in Santa Fe and wants to share a hotel room, or someone I know there will call and ask if I'm going to be in the area any time soon. I will get the "feeling" from my soul that stopping in Amarillo will not deter the mission of getting to Santa Fe and my friend in Amarillo will be home when I call to invite her to dinner. When I leave on the trip to Santa Fe, I may have no idea of what the mission will entail or who I will meet there. My job is to be willing, to show up and to look as good as good As I can. The look good part does not come from my ego. My soul is very clear that how we look determines other's first impressions of us and that, in order for that impression to be positive so the energy moves through us to them, we need to be well groomed.

When I first started working toward becoming a soul infused personality, I carried tremendous anger and sadness in my psyche and body. I was all about being "reactive" to every situation rather than understanding that the purpose of every encounter was to give me an opportunity to allow the soul to "respond" to the situation rather than for me to "react" from my accumulated pain and misconception of how the Universe works. I lived in a defensive posture. I had to be willing to get in the back seat and watch myself, my feelings, my thoughts and to wait before I spoke or acted. The first step in spiritual maturity is to begin to be aware of our thoughts in order to change them to be in alignment with the soul.

I lived in a place of continual melancholy that often moved into depression. I could not see the joy or humor in everyday occurrences, nor was I attuned to the beauty of nature. I was stuck in my preprogramming from childhood. It took years of watching myself and listening to myself to hear why I would react to certain situations in an unreasonable manner. When I began to change, it confused the people who were used to me being a certain way. When I began to live from my intuitive guidance, I was thought to be crazy by my family and friends. My husband at the time actually had me interviewed by three psychologists in an attempt to prove I was insane or emotionally unstable in order to have me committed. (In Texas, if a husband can get three psychologists to agree that a wife is unstable he can get her committed.) Frequently, our changing threatens the reality of those around us, especially those who are not willing to change or to perceive a broader reality than the one they've always known and trusted, even though it may be based on lies or inaccurate information. Many people are simply afraid to experience a fuller revelation of who they are at this time, and their fear may be projected onto you as a concern about your sanity. Instead of defending your beliefs, send them a silent blessing and move on. Your life may seem to be getting crazier at first when you begin to seek your own truth rather than your life seeming to immediately be easier. You may feel overwhelmed at first with how to integrate all the new ideas and understanding you've gained.

Staying grounded while constantly agreeing to funnel more and more Light into this dimension is extremely important. If you do not currently have a grounding process that works for you, you will find that information in this book. Read the chapter on Overcoming being Empathic in Favor of Being Consciously Multi-Dimensional.

The degree to which people hold onto those things that are not of the higher vibration is the degree to which they will experience pain. Misunderstandings and hurts from the past will be surfacing to be healed. Handling what one is accustomed to can seem easier than change. But we are at a point in evolution and energy that is extreme. Nothing happens halfway now, everything is accelerated.

I'm not a fan of astrology, since I've never studied it and don't really understand the language, but every year (once I had made contact with my soul) my soul would suggest that I have a chart and tape done by a wonderful woman who used to live in Oklahoma and now lives in Connecticut. Every year the message would be the same: "You must surrender more." Now, considering that I had surrendered my positions in the church and community, surrendered my security of having a husband, surrendered having a home of my own, had surrendered to go anywhere, do anything, say anything the soul asked of me, you might imagine this message infuriated me. I had no idea what else I could surrender. I had surrendered my body to be used by the soul. At the end of each year, I would take stock of what I had learned and realized gradually what I needed to surrender many times was "the need to know" the need to know beforehand how a situation was going to turn out, the need to know why Spirit wanted my body in Denver or Portland or Santa Fe before I would take the body there. The need to know "why" very often slowed down my progress. Each year I learned to surrender more fear, more resistance, more need to know. The more I surrendered, the more I was allowed to know.

You may want to consider your own personality. What makes you angry? What makes you sad? What makes you happy? What causes you to laugh? What scares you? Asking yourself these questions can also help you to identify your life's purpose. Once we truly understand that we are not our bodies, but are spiritual beings having this Human experience and that this experience was designed to be co-creative and fun, we can let go of much of what we have feared. The ego likes recognition. If we recognize it and give it a say in decisions, but do not allow it to rule our personality, it usually embarrasses us less often and more often we can learn to laugh at ourselves.

Getting all "het" up (that's a Texas expression meaning heated) about politics, the environment, what other people are doing, the state of the World, what your child, mother, spouse or significant other is doing or not doing is all about the ego and is a diversion from what we are to be about. When we are in a state of anger, agitation, disagreement or depression about a situation, we are not in alignment with our soul. We are not letting God drive the limo and it will make us miserable. If only things were different, then I could be happy. Things will not be different until we see them differently. If we look at the big picture of where the World and Humanity are compared to 100 years ago we can see progress.

If we look only at what's wrong, or what we perceive to be wrong, we get more of what we think is wrong. The only way to correct a situation is by looking at our perception of the situation. Other people will never please us 100% of the time. We have a responsibility to ask our souls to show us the big picture. If we look at one small part of what we think is happening on the planet and begin to judge and believe it should be different than it is, we become a part of the problem. We give our energy to the horrors we hear on the BBC news in the middle of the night or the ten o'clock news just before we go to bed. Listening to the news while riding to work, if we believe what is being reported should be other than what it is, it can ruin our whole day, our whole outlook.

We have a responsibility to focus on what's working, what's beautiful, what's good in our lives and in the World. This is not being an ostrich; it is bringing to the situation an energy that is higher than the energy that is currently operating in the circumstance. A problem can never be solved at the level of consciousness it was created. If we focus on a 3D problem with 3D energy, we expand the problem. If we focus on a 3D situation with 5D energy, we can change it or see the truth of what it is about. It is important not to ask for how to fix a problem, because it will need to be fixed again. Do not ask for an answer, because you will then have to figure out how to use the answer. Always ask for the solution which will dissolve the problem

When your spiritual body is stimulated by contact from a higher source, your personality is also stimulated. You want to be able to count on every side of your personality to use its energy to cooperate with your true life's purpose, not to sabotage your efforts and relationships.

# 46.

# Building The Bridge

There is a place that exists in another dimension of reality. It is a highly energized place that has been created by our souls and the Masters. The higher beings of Light are focusing energy and Light on this place day and night. You may choose to see it as a Golden Pyramid, a Crystal Pyramid or a temple. Going to this place in meditation makes it possible for you to receive information from your soul, make changes in relationships, to resolve conflicts and to manifest your heart's desires.

Consider creating a personal bridge in space between you and your pyramid. Consider making the bridge up of the colors of all the Rays of energy coming from the heart of God. Let yourself intention going into meditation and going inside a Golden Pyramid. In your Golden Pyramid, you can raise the frequency of your cellular structure and heal and energize your physical body. This Pyramid is your soul in symbolic form. As you sit or lay in your Pyramid, begin to bring in each God quality and connect it to your body through the apex of the Pyramid. Bring in each quality with your breath. How you breathe strongly influences your energy field, your views and your values. Deepen your breathing and your perception changes. Thoughts become clear instead of scattered or confused. Optimistic feelings start to rise up. Your emotions tend to become calm and positive as breathing slows and the brain waves get longer. Your rhythm of breathing is important because it is a key to activating brain cells and aligning them with the frequency of your soul.

Breathe in each quality, qualities such as compassion, wisdom, love, joy, grace, beauty, courage, forgiveness, clarity, harmony, truth, trust, confidence, humor, oneness, acceptance, patience, perseverance, higher organization, a positive vision of the future, enthusiasm, serenity, understanding and peace. You may see the qualities come in as colors or you may just feel the energy. Remember, seeing is a slower form of spiritual energy, hearing is the next higher form and knowingness is an even higher form of energy. Go for the silence, go for knowingness.

Once you have established contact with your Pyramid through intention, you may take any question there and ask it of your soul. If you have someone with whom you are not in agreement, invite them silently (through intention) to join you in their etheric body in your Pyramid. At this level, have a conversation with the individual or group with whom you have trouble communicating Third dimensionally. From your Pyramid you can tune the dials to the soul and send a message to any individual you wish, to a group such as the children of the World, or all of Humanity. If you do not know what message to send, you might consider this: "Live fully and in peace. Love your life. Be joyful. You are free to live from the authority of your own soul."

Communicating with someone in your Golden Pyramid does not take away their Freewill. You are inviting them into a relationship of Light and Love. From your Pyramid you can reach anyone anywhere in the Universe. Deliberately calling forth leaders of the World into your Pyramid for conversation, to encourage loving understanding between people, even if they have different beliefs and goals, can work miracles. We have a responsibility to use all these techniques Spirit gives us to make this evolution of Earth and Humanity quicker and easier. Within the Pyramid there is no sense of time, so you can resolve conflicts that you hold in your energy field even with people who are no longer in this dimension.

Your first act of courage was to be born onto planet Earth in a Human body. Your courage to now bring in higher vibrations of energy, and to express greater wisdom and love, powerfully affects many people, including many you may never meet. True courage results in a steady and persistent intelligent action to bring about what has true value to you. <u>Each time you act with courage, you empower your entire life</u>. Every time you act from courage, you strengthen your ability to live by the authority of your own soul. You empower others who can see the positive direction and purpose of your courage. <u>Be a living example of vitality and creativity. Courage is easier when you have a sense of real purpose</u>.

Getting in touch with your purpose for being here, beyond raising your vibration and the vibration of Earth and Humanity, is easier when you think of the things you loved to do as a child. Did you build things? Did you organize the kids in the neighborhood into a club? Did you draw on the sidewalk? Did you spend your time with a book in your face, as I did?

Did you make up stories? Did you play an instrument? Did you work jigsaw puzzles? Did you throw Frisbees?

One man in a class realized that what he was good at and loved to do was to throw Frisbees. He thought of taking his skill to other countries and teaching other people to do what he loved. He got a grant from the United Nations to make a thousand Frisbees with the emblem of the World on each disk. The grant included enough for him to make a trip to Russia to distribute the peace symbols of One World, One People, and gave him an opportunity to interact with people of a different culture doing something fun. His love of playing Frisbee caused him to become a peace ambassador. What do you love?

Take time to think; don't fill your hours with sound and activity that override your ability to hear your thoughts. What you think creates the quality of your life. If you listen to the radio, television, or other people, your quality of life is influenced by people who normally do not have your highest good in mind. They ether want to sell you something, want you to join with them in some kind of activity that is against something or want you to vote to give "them" more power. Make sure you are the one using your mind. Your mind is your most precious gift. Your mind and what you put into it creates your reality. Spend time in your Golden Pyramid. Invite scholars, inventors, composers, artists from the past whom you admire, to join you there. Ask their advice. They will join you and they will help you. All of the Masters of the Renaissance are now available to help us through this difficult period. We have access to so much help if we remember to ask.

# 47.

# Our Emotions And Beliefs Affect Manifestation

The relationship between our inner Worlds of consciousness and outer Worlds of "objective reality" is the opposite of what our culture teaches. Our World is a reflection and "effect" of Human thought. Human thought is the "cause." The World is not there to create struggle, victimize us, block spiritual progress, or provide us with excuses for our unhappiness. It is there to provide a stage or medium through which all of the dramas of consciousness, from agony to ecstasy, can be played out and reflected upon. Once one grasps this fundamental inversion, whether it manifests in the form of repressed anger crystallizing as a tumor, as in my breast cancer, or your boss failing to acknowledge your contributions at work, your spouse or partner not appreciating your efforts, the door is open to many paths of growth. Without this realization, the chances of becoming stuck in places we don't want to be are significantly increased. Once we realize what we think is what we get, what we think with intense feeling we get to experience even quicker.

    In my case I recently became aware that I do not attract male relationships that are with men who are balanced. I have held very negative opinions and beliefs about the male Human population. When I consciously recognized the belief and the result, I wondered how do I manifest something I don't believe exists or something I've never seen. The soul threw a book off the shelf to get my attention. The book suggested that instead of praying for something that I didn't believe existed, I should pray to be healed of my negative beliefs about men in general. As a result of the prayer my primary care physician, who of course happens to be a male, refused to continue to be my physician unless I agreed to a complete physical. While feeling as if I was being held hostage by a male dominated system (the medical system) I resented it, but agreed to the physical; it was easier than changing doctors. I consider myself to be a healthy person, but I needed prescriptions for estrogen, since I've had my internal female organs removed and I need a script for thyroid meds, because I push way too much energy through my pituitary and pineal glands doing the work I do and this affects my thyroid function. I have to have a medical doctor to get these meds.

During the physical the doctor noticed a lump in my left breast, my female side. He made an appointment for me to have a mammogram, which led to a breast biopsy, which led to an MRI, which led to a male surgeon, which led to surgery. The male surgeon is one of the most "present" medical professionals I've ever met. He truly had my highest good in mind, treated me as if I am intelligent, listened and explained everything in great detail in easy to understand terms. It was obvious <u>he had no ego need to seem superior to me. I was amazed</u>.

The second I heard the diagnosis "it is cancer" I mentally made the agreement with my soul that I would do whatever treatments were necessary without fear, but I would not pay for the treatments myself. After I put my clothes back on, I walked into the lobby of the clinic. A woman walked up to me and asked me if I had time to speak with her for a few minutes. I followed her into her office. She was the financial officer of the clinic. She asked me about my income and my occupation. After I described my circumstances, she said she felt she could intervene to get me set up with Medicaid for at least a year which would pay all the expenses of my treatments, which she did. Making agreements with our soul about our desires is an important part of manifestation.

I immediately kept an appointment I had made previously with friends to meet in Denver to celebrate the New Year and to do some energy work on the Rocky Mountain Fault Line. While I was there a male chiropractor and healer I have not seen in over fifteen years called and offered to help me get to the core belief that created the circumstances for the tumor to live in my body. He had changed completely since the last time I had seen him. His ego had diminished to the point that being in the same room with him was comfortable. He had reached a point of allowing his soul to give him intuitive assistance. He muscle tested me in a very awkward position so that my mental attitude could not mask the results of my body giving him accurate answers. He immediately learned from my body that that the stage had been set for the negative belief and mistrust of males had happened at the age of nine in this body and that at the soul level the events being healed happened during the time of the Knights Templar. After the energetic release work we accomplished I immediately felt lighter, but the tumor was still there.

I returned to Oklahoma City. The surgeon accomplished the surgery and I recovered with no pain. I've had lumpectomies before for fibroid cysts and the after effect pain was excruciating. A friend who is a retired nurse volunteered to stay with me for 48 hours after the surgery, which was a great help.

Two weeks later I had an appointment with a male oncologist. He felt there was a discrepancy between the pathology report on the biopsied material and the material from the actual tumor that was sent for pathology testing. These materials were sent to be retested. The oncologist was sure I needed severe chemotherapy followed by six weeks of radiation. Since I still didn't feel I had signed up for anything beyond surgery and radiation I was amazed when I was taken into the chemotherapy room and could see myself sitting in one of the chairs talking with other patients. Through the years I've been consciously working with the soul, one of the things I've trained myself to do is to project myself into the future to see if I can see myself in the possible situation, such as attending a conference, traveling to another city or country or attending a party. If I can see myself there in the projection I know I will be there and I begin to make plans accordingly.

After the biopsy proved the lump was cancer I agreed to the surgery and radiation, but still felt I would not have to have chemotherapy. The biopsy and surgery had already taken two months. The chemo was to take another six months and the radiation another six weeks. I could not imagine giving over nine months of my life to this experience. I renegotiated with my soul in meditation. I've just heard back from the oncologist that he feels I can do with a lower form of chemotherapy, which would only take six weeks, then radiation for six weeks. Next week I went in for another surgery to have a port installed in my chest through which the chemotherapy will be administered.

When I was diagnosed I was amazed and asked the soul, why do I have this? The response was that at the level of my soul I have agreed to have breast cancer and to use both allopathic and alternative methods to correct this imbalance for myself and for Humanity without fear. The fear of cancer and especially breast cancer is high in Human consciousness at this time. For a person to have the dis-ease and to walk through the procedures without fear and to add this to Human consciousness is important. When one Human does a supposedly impossible thing it enters a matrix into Human consciousness that makes it possible for others to accomplish the same task if they choose. I have to admit, however, even though I didn't feel fear, I did feel inconvenienced. When the recommended procedures were mammogram, sonogram, biopsy, surgery, radiation I was able to feel it was a minor inconvenience. Once the treatment procedures were expanded I began to feel it was a major inconvenience. The doctors were all males.

The Earth's frequency is speeding up and things that used to happen slowly and with little intensity are now hitting us fast and hard. The more condensed the energy around and within the Earth becomes the less time it takes for our negative or positive thoughts to express themselves as our reality. The current rash of natural disasters and Earth changes that we see in the news everyday is proof of that. We won't be able to pull together collectively to live in the Aquarian Age if enough individuals don't decide to start on their own path of personal growth. <u>Personal paths must lead away from fear and isolation toward the chance to bring personal power to bear on the problems that face us all.</u>

Matter is really energy. We may know Einstein's famous formula $E=mc2$, but we don't really believe that the World works that way. Metaphysics really is putting the idea that everything is energy into everyday use in our lives. Energy has flow, usually cyclical. It wants to move. Example: electricity can't stand still; it exists only as an electrical current. In our energy fields we see this manifested as the eternal cycle of giving and receiving and the internal cycle of growth and manifestations. Energy has polarity: +/-, yin/yang, odd/even. In our energy fields we see this manifested as male and female. An energy field has magnetism – it draws like things to it. Examples: gravity, an electromagnet. This is how we create our own reality. Energy seeks balance. Example: a bolt of lightning will always try to ground itself. We can see this in our own energy fields. This balance will become external if there is no internal balance. For instance, a person who gets their sense of worth from taking care of others will usually end up marrying or attracting people who want or need to be taken care of.

Everything is energy and therefore we are energy. The physical form that we think of as our "body" is really four separate energy fields overlaid on top of each other. These four energy fields are the physical, the emotional, the mental and the spiritual. Each one is centered around a focused energy point called a "chakra." There is a physical chakra, an emotional chakra, a mental chakra, a spiritual chakra. These four energy centers, or points, are sort of central "clearing houses" for energy flowing through the body that they represent. That is to say that if, for instance, there is going to be a blockage of energy flow, or "log jam," through the emotional body, the emotional chakra is probably where it will first become evident. Since the emotional chakra is located just below the navel, this blockage might manifest itself as a physical tightening of the muscles in that area or even a constriction in the digestive flow: i.e. a bout of constipation.

There are seven major chakras, the four "lower" chakras, and the three "higher" chakras: the power center in the throat, the "third eye" in the forehead, and the crown chakra on top of the head. The four lower chakras are related to our physical reality, the upper three are more attached to that part of us that is independent of this present incarnation, the soul.

All energies have a specific frequency or vibration. For example, a specific frequency of Light would be a particular color, a specific frequency of sound would be a particular pitch or note. Our energy fields are spectrums, with each chakra being a specific frequency in that spectrum. Our "souls," or "higher selves" – or whatever term you prefer—is that highest and most energetic frequency of that spectrum, and our physical bodies are the lowest, densest, and slowest frequency.

Anything that is energy has a specific rate of vibration; this is called its frequency. Remember energy is in constant motion. If something has a frequency it has a sound and a color. Only very small portions of those frequencies fall into ranges in the two scales that our eyes and ears can pick up. Since our energy fields are a collection of different frequencies, like "white" Light, they can also be broken down into these same colors. Red is at the bottom end of the rainbow because it has the lowest frequency (travels at the slowest vibration). So, the color red corresponds to our densest and slowest aspect: the physical.

The chakra for the physical body is at the base of the spine in the groin/tailbone region, and it would be red. The emotional chakra is located right below the navel in front of the sacrum bone of your spine and its color is orange. The mental chakra is in the solar plexus right below the sternum and its color is yellow. The spiritual chakra is in the center of the chest, in our heart space and its color is green. The throat chakra, which is our center of power and communication, is blue. The "third eye" or psychic center in the middle of the brain, which we think of as reflected into the forehead, is indigo. Our connection to our higher self is considered the "crown" chakra and is violet.

The important concept to grasp is that Human beings are not just static lumps of matter. We are made of energy fields that affect, and are affected by, the rest of the World. Our energy fields have several different levels that interact with each other and our surroundings. Our physical bodies, then, are just the hard, innermost kernel of an onion-like energy field that floats in the sea of energy that makes up our reality. Our bodies are energy fields. Matter is energy. We are matter. Energy has a flow, therefore we have a flow. A healthy body is the manifestation of a flowing energy field. A blocked or stagnant energy field will manifest as an injury or disease. An affliction of the physical body is caused by a block in our energy field, held in place by an emotion.

But what about accidents, such as dropping a hammer on your foot, how can that be caused by a blocked energy field? If you hold your arm near the energy field of the television screen, the hairs all stand up. That shows that energy fields affect their environment. We know that energy has this "magnetic" property. So if your field contained the belief (an energy) that you couldn't stand up for what was rightfully yours, held in place by the fear of confronting your boss about a raise? Couldn't that magnetically draw an accident to the part of your body that symbolically represents standing?

If everything is energy, then God or the Universe or whatever your idea of perfection is, is also energy. So, as energy beings, we are all part of that perfection. We are all made of the same energy as the rest of the Universe (God included), so we are all connected.

When I say we are all made of the same energy, I am not implying that we have no differences. For instance, the Atlantic and Pacific Oceans are obviously connected and made up of the exact same substance, water. But they have many different characteristics: direction of currents, frequency of storms, temperature, etc. Because they are different expressions of the same thing, we think of them as separate entities; as energy beings, we are the same way. If we accept this concept of connectedness, it makes it much easier to imagine that changes in our energy fields would lead to changes in the flow of energy that is creating the circumstances in our lives. Raising the water temperature in the Atlantic by even a few degrees would eventually affect the quantity and quality of marine life in the Pacific.

The earlier example about the raise and the hammer, would be ludicrous for a being that is part of the perfection of the Creator to not have the strength or the right to stand up for what they deserve. So, we see that a block in energy flow is really an "untruth" that blocks the energy flowing through our energy field. "I'm not good enough, handsome enough, beautiful enough, smart enough," "I can't get what I need," "I'll always be alone," etc.—are really just variations of the central "untruth" that we are not part of the perfection of God energy. We hold these untruths in all four of our bodies, physical, emotional, mental and spiritual, all the time, and the manifestation of these blocks into our World causes us much pain and suffering.

Whatever we are holding in our energy fields, truths or untruths, flow or stagnation, is what we create (manifest) in our lives. Our energy fields are the pattern or blueprint of what actually percolates down into the densest and lowest energy level or vibration, the physical reality that we all know.

If a person is holding an untruth in their field (held in place by fear) that says "When things are going good for me, something bad always happens." Say, this person just got a raise at work. Guess what? They try to make a left hand turn through traffic, and the person going the other way just happens to be holding an untruth in their energy field (held in place by guilt) that says "I'm not a trustworthy person." Sure enough, this person is driving a car they borrowed from their Mother. If an accident happens; is it Fate, predestination, Will of God, random coincidence, or two corresponding energy fields working together to draw in a situation that will play out both of those beliefs? If we believe that the very fabric of the Universe is energy first and matter second, a situation being drawn together and created by energy is not hard to imagine. <u>Energy is where everything starts and matter is the result</u>. Neither of the people in the accident consciously chose to get in an accident, therefore they can easily take the role of victim rather than to own up to their position as creators of their own reality.

Our untruths can be very deeply buried in our unconscious, yet they are still in our energy field, and they are forming the blueprint from which we create our reality. It is much simpler to chalk it up to "bad luck" and take the other guy to court. Taking that position, however, means that those unconsciously held (and untrue) beliefs will continue to play out in our lives.

Using the analogy of a river, the general shape and course of the river stays petty constant as you look at it from minute to minute (although it changes in the long run), but the water running past you at any given minute is not the same water that was there the minute before. That particular water is quite a ways downstream. Our energy fields are the same way. When everything is going as it should, we are merely the completion of a circuit that connects us to our Higher Self or the Universe. So it is the pattern that the energy flows through, and not the actual energy, that forms what we see.

These "patterns" that channel the energy are our beliefs about who we are and how the World works. Although at some level we hold them to be gospel, these beliefs may, as we have seen, bear little resemblance to the real Truth: we are all part of the same energy as God, the Creator or Perfection. We, like the river, must have flow. If part of the river's current gets diverted from its perfection (onward flow), that water will form a stagnant pool or eddy. Mosquitoes begin to breed there. Sticks, garbage, and other debris begin to build up, and soon a logjam or block is formed. We are the same way. If we are holding a pattern that deviates from our truth of Perfection, then we get blocked, and stagnant places in our energy field will soon begin to manifest as a physical disease, accident or a diseased life situation pattern, such as attracting relationships with people who are afraid of commitment.

A flowing energy field is a healthy energy field. Our energy fields are sometimes cluttered with other things: mental chatter, stray emotions that aren't stuck (we just forgot to let go of them), even unacknowledged physical needs. It helps to get this energetic "clutter" out of the way before trying to deal with our deep-seated programming or blocks. Meditation is a great tool for clearing ourselves. Regardless of the form your meditation takes, it can help you to release the "static," the random energy that is cluttering up your energy field.

Breathing in and out is a flow of energy. The breath is a very effective way to physically do something to move energy. Thoughts are also energy. Using our Imagination we can add energy to the nerve pathways that will soon carry out any action we have planned. Breath and imagination are two of the most powerful tools for clearing our energy field. You may want to read this portion of the exercise into a tape recorder to use for yourself.

After you have entered meditation through your own method of intention and breath, begin to breathe deliberately into the chakra at the base of your tailbone. Let the breath expand it like blowing on the embers of a fire. See its red color grow brighter and brighter. Don't force it, let the breath activate and begin to feel the energy resonate throughout your physical body. Let physical tensions flow out with your outgoing breath. Feel your shoulders and other chronic tension areas relax. Let your physical body begin to speak to you. It might say something like, "I'm hungry, this seat cushion feels lumpy or it's really warm in this room." Acknowledge each of these messages and then let them go. Breathe them out.

When the physical chakra feels fully activated and each of its voices has been heard and allowed to release, let the breath draw the energy up to your second chakra, the emotional. See it as a ball of energy located just below your navel. Breathe into this point of light which is the center of your emotional body and let it expand, its orange color getting brighter and brighter. Let any emotional voices that need to speak, be heard. "I'm still mad at my sister-in-law for that cheap birthday gift." "I'm worried about all the bills this month." Don't try to fix them, just acknowledge that they are there and let them go. See them float up and out with your breath into your soul, into your I AM Presence. If one emotion screams for attention, reassure it that you will come back to it later and let it float on out so that your emotional space can be clear.

When the emotional chakra feels fully activated and each of its voices has been heard and allowed to release, let the breath draw the energy up to your third chakra, the mental. See it as a glowing point of energy in your solar plexus, just below your "wishbone." As you visualize the yellow color of this chakra, feel the energy field of the surrounding mental body begin to quiet down. Let each of the stray thoughts that come up flow across your internal screen and off the other side. Acknowledge them, but don't let them draw you into conversation. "I wonder if I cleaned out my In-box at work?" "What are we having for dinner?" Breathe them up and out into your soul, your I AM Presence, clearing the space within the body.

When each of the three lower bodies has been cleared and activated, turn your attention to the Heart chakra, the center point of your spiritual body. Imagine it in the center of your chest as a green spark of energy. Breathe into it and see how the breath connects it to the lower three chakras like pearls on a string. As the spiritual body is cleared and activated like the lower three, with each of its voices being acknowledged and released, let the breath strengthen the ribbon of energy that connects them all. Feel it grow into a pole of light that runs all the way through the center of your body. Let any cares or sorrows that are weighing heavily on your heart be whisked up and out with your breath.

Complete the process by extending this shaft of energy up through your neck and out through the top of your head, clearing and activating the three upper chakras along the way: the sky blue throat chakra in your neck; the indigo colored psychic chakra, or the "third eye" in your forehead; and the violet colored crown chakra at the top of your head. See once again how they are all connected like pearls on a string by the stream of energy that now runs all the way through you. Feel how this beam of light connects you through your feet to the central core energy of the Earth and through the crown of your head to your soul, your I AM Presence.

Your energy field is now clean and flowing, visualize an egg-shaped envelope of pure White Light that surrounds you and prevents outside energies from flowing into the internal spaces you have created. Meditating and clearing your chakras first can prepare a "blank slate" as you prepare to tackle those deep seated patterns that are blocking your growth.

We each create our individual reality, collectively we create our society. We each contain both male and female energies. Sadly, our male and female parts often do not work together, and are, in fact, openly antagonistic at times. We've gone through history with matriarchy and patriarchy. It is time for an Age of balance, what Spirit calls androgenarchy. Everything that is happening in our society today, everything that's manifesting, is a direct result of what is happening internally with people.

Child abuse is suddenly exposed publically. Child abuse is not a new thing, but enough individuals have done their internal work to break the cycle. Their parents had an internal imbalance of discipline (masculine energy) and nurturing (feminine energy). They expressed it externally by hurting their kids, but the kids refuse to pass it on.

When we become aware of a block energetically, or an untruth held in consciousness, we can reprogram it. Everything we need and desire is actually energy. "I need money right now," actually means "I need the energy of abundance that money represents for me." All these "things" that we think we need in order to be fulfilled and happy, can really all be boiled down to a specific energy or energies.

We are, as energy beings, made in the image and likeness of God, which means we are the same energy as the Creator and Creation. Therefore, all the various energies found in God can be found within ourselves. We have all those energies within us, but we have to learn how to access them and use them so we can begin to manifest all the "things" we need or desire.

First look at your life and determine if you have a need that is going unmet. Agree to uncover within yourself the untruth that keeps what you desire from being your reality. In the growth cycle, our emotions serve as our teachers. If you have a need that is not being met, you will have an emotion. Emotional pain and distress are little red flags that say "Warning: you have a need that is not being met."

If I remain conscious:
    An event happens.
    I have an emotional response.
    I ask, "What is my need here?"
    I become aware an energy, from my heart (my soul),
    that would meet my need is now available to me.

With this realization I have grown.
I now have a new quality available in my heart.
I can plan a course of action to express this soul quality.
That action will be supported by a positive feeling
I will now manifest new events in my life.

For example, if someone capitalizes on my idea at work and receives praise from the boss that I feel should rightfully have been mine, I may feel anger. The anger tells me that I have a need going unmet. That is all. Not that I should retaliate in any way, just that I have a need that is going unmet. I was not receiving the energy that I needed from that interaction. Maybe the energy was honor. If the emotion I felt in the same situation was fear. I might be afraid that my co-worker would appear smarter and more efficient to my boss and that I would soon be out of a job. An energy, other than honor, is missing. It is important to determine, what are you not getting? Suppose the co-worker is a friend and the emotion you felt was betrayal. Any of these feelings lets you know you are not holding in your energy field, the energy necessary to magnetically draw in what you want or desire.

If our needs are not being met, we will experience pain. Emotional pain at first (fear, guilt, anger and grief are a few), but if we push the feeling away and do not let it express on the emotional level it will eventually become a physical pain.

Our job then, is to listen to our emotional pain and see where it takes us. The biggest obstacle to this is, owning our emotions. We must constantly remind ourselves that "this emotion is for me and about me." If we fall into the victim of believing that "you made me angry" (or sad, or upset, etc.) or "you caused my pain," then all growth is lost. We will never get to the bottom of our feeling because we just gave it away. If you caused me to be angry, then it is not my anger, it is yours.

If you yell at me, I can feel any one of a number of things, ranging from annoyance that you interrupted my chain of thought, to elation that you finally got that off your chest and now the air is clear. If I end up feeling angry about the yelling, it is because I chose that feeling from a wide range of possibilities. That is the key, if I chose the feeling there is a reason. Staying with our emotions about a particular situation long enough to own them and following them to the "Why" is the first step in the personal growth cycle. The door to awareness is through emotion.

Behind every feeling is a piece of you saying "I want to express." Not,

"I want to tell them off, but "I want to express me for me." Life really is all about you.

Many feelings are uncomfortable enough that we want to make the pain go away as quickly as possible. So we take a little taste of them and then quickly shove them back down, or onto someone else. This doesn't move them out of the way, and we don't get the issue (the "Why") that is behind the feeling. However, if we can stay with the emotions long enough – not judging it, not pushing it away, just sitting right in the middle of it – then it begins to detach itself from the situation or other person and begins to reveal something about us. Instead of "you made me angry by yelling at me," it becomes "when you yelled, I became angry because _____."

That empty blank is our "Why" and we may have to repeat that statement over and over to ourselves, letting the blank space just hang there, but eventually something will come up to fill it. When it does, we have our answer. "When you yelled, I became angry because...I was scared and my anger feels protective to me."

There may be several layers to our answer, but we keep asking "why" until we get to the rock bottom. You'll know you've reached the bottom when all you have left is a statement about who you are. Why did I get scared when you yelled? Because "I don't feel safe when other people express themselves with intensity." There! Rock bottom. A statement about who I am. I am a person who lacks the energy of safety in this situation. If you have uncovered the issue behind your emotion, there will always be an energy missing. Remember, that is what the emotion is all about – a need going unmet – and needs are energies, not "things."

Once you have stayed with the emotion long enough to detach it from the circumstances and get to the "Why," the second step is to replace the untruth ("I lack safety") with your truth (I am made of the same energy as God, Perfection, my I AM Presence. I most certainly do have the energy of safety in me, and I can bring it to bear in any situation I choose.").

The physical is the actual event, the yelling. The emotional is being aware of the feelings. The mental is holding focus for long enough to get to the rock bottom belief. So that leaves the spiritual body. Our Spirit is the sum total of all the qualities that make us up: our compassion, our love, our sense of adventure and play, our capacity for sharing, to name a few. So when I say "I am made of the same energy as God and I do have the energy of safety in me somewhere" – that somewhere is our spiritual body, centered in our heart chakra. We are made of the same energy as God. Our spiritual bodies contain all the same energies, qualities as God. The problem is that we have not claimed very many of those energies as our own. We generally are hanging on to a multitude of untruths that assert such things as "I am not enough," "I cannot have safety," or "I don't deserve."

The first step in the growth cycle is an awareness of your need. The second step is claiming your truth. Tune in to your spiritual body the same way you did to your emotional body. Breathe into your heart, your spiritual chakra. Speak into that spiritual space, "I need safety." You will feel an energy response. The energy of safety will begin to be sent to you from your soul. Claim the energy. "I AM part of the energy of God and I do have the energy of safety in me and I can call it forth whenever I choose." If you have never had safety in your life before, the energy may feel unfamiliar and elusive. Part of the process then, is sitting in the middle of that energy, just like you did the emotion, until you know the feel of it inside and out. When we claim a new part of ourselves in this way, we have expanded our energy field. This is true growth.

Try going back through your day (or week) and bring to mind situations in which you were aware of a strong emotional response. Then go through the growth cycle process with each one. Follow the process through your four bodies. Physical: an event happens. Be aware: Is this really about me? What are my reactions?

Then there is the emotional: How do I feel about this? "I choose to feel this way because_____?" Our job is to stay focused through all the layers of "Why" until we get to the need at the rock bottom... the statement of who we are around the event.

Then there is the spiritual: what energy or quality could I incorporate into my field that would meet this need?

If you visualize this progression as a flow chart through your four bodies and their corresponding chakras, you will notice that the flow of this cycle is upward. The growth cycle is about following the energy of a situation up from the lowest and densest vibration of our spectrum to the highest and most energetic.

You will probably also notice that the Male aspects of our energy field, the physical and mental, play a rather passive role in the growth cycle – awareness and focus. Our Female side provides the activity during this part of the cycle – the discovery of our need (emotional) and the claiming of our truth (spiritual). If our Male and Female aspects are out of balance, we can get stuck at some point in the process and just keep repeating one segment instead of growing beyond it. For example: If a person is most comfortable in their mental body and allows that body to be overactive;

it will try to and take charge and the male energy will be out of balance. They may not be able to maintain a focus long enough to get through all the layers of emotion and find the real need. If that is the case, the cycle stops right there and the same issue keeps coming up in that person's life. They continue to have the same emotional reactions and get discouraged that they can't seem to break out of this pattern.

If your physical response is to "do something" or "fix the situation" before you can even be with the emotion and get to the need, then the physical body is too active and is probably getting in the way of your awareness. Calm down the physical body. Go back to the beginning of the process and make an effort to remain aware. Focus on each body individually, step by step. Is each body doing its job?

Growth is endless. We learn a small piece of who we are, manifest that piece, and that will lead us to a new lesson or another aspect of the same lesson that we didn't get the first time. Remember life is a game. Learn to play without taking every event personally, other than how does it provide an opportunity for me to grow, for me to learn more about myself?

If we make a prayer, which is expressed on a higher frequency, it can make a change on one end of the spectrum, eventually percolating down into a lower vibration (the physical or mental body) as a large or perceptible change.

Am I healed of my negative beliefs about the Males of our species and my own Maleness? No, but I'm making progress. The more I agree to be healed, both in my own Maleness and in my attitudes, the more possible it has become for me to be physically and emotionally healed and for me to bring Males into my life that are conscious, ego diminished and helpful. When I heal my beliefs, I can heal my body.

Whatever it is you desire you must become this in your mind, words, feelings, desires, and actions. Act as if, and you are. The outer must correspond to the inner.

## 48.

# People Who Do Not Have Personal Goals Are Doomed To Work For Those Who Do

It is important to write and read our intentions in present tense, because they describe our desired results, our intended life. If we state them in the present tense we are more likely to work to do the next single thing toward accomplishing them now rather than holding them in future context.

I now accept...
I AM now experiencing...
I AM now enjoying...
I AM now grateful for...

Example: I AM now accepting a life filled with joy, adventure, love, beauty, friends, fun and health, with money and time in excess of my needs and desires.

Read your affirmations daily with enthusiasm and emotion. You are sending these messages into your sub-conscious mind to replace the erroneous messages you've held there with your new truth. You are sending these "purchase orders" into the Universe to be acted out to the highest good of all concerned in alignment with the Divine Plan of the Creator.

You may want to write them on 3x5 cards and carry them with you to read anytime you have to wait or to keep a set in the drawer of your desk at work or write them on your computer. You may choose to make a poster of words and pictures that place these desires into your sub-conscious visually. You can also do this in a notebook form. I do all of the above and it has changed my life. We can argue that all that would take too much time, but I can assure you it is time well spent. Writing it out, in as much detail as possible, gives your soul a blueprint of what you desire. It also gives them permission to help you to achieve it. It keeps you focused on action rather than living your life passively, sitting back waiting for the next two by four.

In my case when I breathed and got in touch with my true heart's desire I had to let go of who I thought I was and what I assumed my life was about. I had to give up the familiar for the unknown. In the beginning my goal setting was vague. At that time I could not even begin to imagine the life I have co-created now. I had to begin with what I could believe. Life is a process. Goal setting is a process and can be an ever-changing process. Sometimes after living with an intention for a while I find it isn't truly what I desire and I change or replace it. Setting intentions gives our lives direction, without which we have a tendency to wander around unfocused or to stay in familiar ruts.

For our lives to become different we have to first be able to imagine or pretend (pre-intend) ourselves in different circumstances performing different roles intentionally from our "I AM", our God Selves, our hearts. It is important to remember we are always playing roles. The trick is to write your own script, choose your own costumes, and choose the other characters with whom you want to share this stage of your life. Allow the "I AM" Self to play the role through you by staying in touch with that I AM part of you, by staying deliberately connected to your soul through your heart.

# 49.

# Precipitation Meditation Steps

1. I deliberately seal this room on the north, south, east and west. I seal the ceiling and the floor against any negative influence or entity. I deliberately fill this room with the blue light of protection.
2. I call forth and ask for the assistance of the Master Saint Germain and the Violet Flame of Transmutation. I ask the Violet Flame to move through my body and consciousness to transmute any beliefs I hold in limitation or doubt of my abilities to manifest my true heart's desires.
3. I call on the Law of Forgiveness to forgive all my mistakes, discord, problems, and limitations, and also those of all Humankind.
4. Breathing deeply, I feel my emotions calming. I feel serene. I feel myself at one with God, at one with the Universe.
5. I decree: I consciously enter and abide within the Heart of the Sacred Fire—the true center of my Being.
6. I AM the Presence of God within the Heart of the Sacred Fire and I speak and command with authority.
7. I AM vested with the Power of the Three times Three. (Repeat X3)
8. I AM vested with the Power of Transmutation. (Repeat X3)
9. I AM vested with the Power of Precipitation. (Repeat X3)
10. I AM vested with the Power of Levitation. Repeat X3)
11. I invoke the assistance of the Elemental Kingdom and the energy of Mercury to speed my manifestation.
12. "LET THERE BE LIGHT, I call forth a cloud of undefined infinite energy into a diameter of nine feet around me to intensify my energy field."
13. I now design a mental matrix of what I desire to precipitate. I see the size, color, proportions, substance, density and details of my desire.
14. I state where I wish the manifestation to appear.
15. I ask the Universal Mind to install, within the vision of my desire, the

correct chemical formula for what I desire to create. I visualize the perfection of my design and ask God to correct and perfect any details I have omitted in my design.

16. In the Name of the Presence of God which "I AM" – through the Magnetic Power of the Sacred Fire vested in me I command the appearance of my desire manifested through the Divine Right Action of God now. When you have the visualization clear in your mind state, "IT IS FINISHED! Not my will, but God's will be done." And thereby release the design to the Elementals and the Builders of Form.

**<u>Concentration and perseverance are important. Don't give up.</u>**

www.ingramcontent.com/pod-product-compliance
Lightning Source LLC
Chambersburg PA
CBHW020356170426
43200CB00005B/195